Wolf Packs

By the Editors of Time-Life Books

Alexandria, Virginia

TIME
LIFE ®

Time-Life Books Inc.
is a wholly owned subsidiary of

The Time Inc. Book Company

President and Chief Executive Officer:
Kelso F. Sutton
President, Time Inc. Books Direct:
Christopher T. Linen

Time-Life Books Inc.

EDITOR: George Constable
Executive Editor: Ellen Phillips
Director of Design: Louis Klein
Director of Editorial Resources: Phyllis K. Wise
Editorial Board: Russell B. Adams, Jr., Dale M.
Brown, Roberta Conlan, Thomas H. Flaherty,
Lee Hassig, Jim Hicks, Donia Ann Steele,
Rosalind Stubenberg
Director of Photography and Research:
John Conrad Weiser

PRESIDENT: John M. Fahey, Jr.
Senior Vice Presidents: Robert M. DeSena, James
L. Mercer, Paul R. Stewart, Curtis G. Viebranz,
Joseph J. Ward
Vice Presidents: Stephen L. Bair, Bonita L.
Boezeman, Stephen L. Goldstein, Juanita T.
James, Andrew P. Kaplan, Trevor Lunn, Susan J.
Maruyama, Robert H. Smith
Supervisor of Quality Control: James King

PUBLISHER: Joseph J. Ward

The Third Reich

SERIES DIRECTOR: Thomas H. Flaherty
Series Administrator: Jane Edwin
Editorial Staff for *Wolf Packs:*
Designer: Raymond Ripper
Picture Editor: Jane Coughran
Text Editors: John Newton, Henry Woodhead
Senior Writer: Stephen G. Hyslop
Researchers: Philip Brandt George, Paula
York-Soderlund (principals); Karen Monks,
Trudy Pearson
Assistant Designers: Alan Pitts, Lorraine D. Rivard
Copy Coordinator: Charles J. Hagner
Picture Coordinators: Ruth Moss,
Robert H. Wooldridge, Jr.
Editorial Assistant: Jayne A. L. Dover,
Patricia D. Whiteford

Special Contributors: Ronald H. Bailey, Lydia
Preston Hicks, Thomas A. Lewis, Milton
Orshefsky, David S. Thomson (text); Martha-Lee
Beckington, Robin Currie, Ann-Louise Gates
(research); Michael Kalen Smith (index)

Editorial Operations
Copy Chief: Diane Ullius
Production: Celia Beattie
Library: Louise D. Forstall

Computer Composition: Gordon E. Buck
(Manager), Deborah G. Tait, Monika D. Thayer,
Janet Barnes Syring, Lillian Daniels

Correspondents: Elisabeth Kraemer-Singh
(Bonn); Christina Lieberman (New York); Maria
Vincenza Aloisi (Paris); Ann Natanson (Rome).
Valuable assistance was also provided by: Lesley
Coleman, Barbara Hicks (London); Elizabeth
Brown (New York); Ann Wise (Rome).

Other Publications:

AMERICAN COUNTRY
VOYAGE THROUGH THE UNIVERSE
THE TIME-LIFE GARDENER'S GUIDE
MYSTERIES OF THE UNKNOWN
TIME FRAME
FIX IT YOURSELF
FITNESS, HEALTH & NUTRITION
SUCCESSFUL PARENTING
HEALTHY HOME COOKING
UNDERSTANDING COMPUTERS
LIBRARY OF NATIONS
THE ENCHANTED WORLD
THE KODAK LIBRARY OF CREATIVE PHOTOGRAPHY
GREAT MEALS IN MINUTES
THE CIVIL WAR
PLANET EARTH
COLLECTOR'S LIBRARY OF THE CIVIL WAR
THE EPIC OF FLIGHT
THE GOOD COOK
WORLD WAR II
HOME REPAIR AND IMPROVEMENT
THE OLD WEST

For information on and a full description of any
of the Time-Life Books series listed above, please
call 1-800-621-7026 or write:
Reader Information
Time-Life Customer Service
P.O. Box C-32068
Richmond, Virginia 23261-2068

The Cover: Lookouts search for targets from the
bridge of a U-boat slicing through choppy water on
the ocean's surface—where World War II submarines spent most of their time. Between 1939 and
1945, Germany's sea wolves sank 14 million tons of
merchant shipping and no fewer than 175 Allied
naval vessels. The U-boats' success moved Winston
Churchill to call them "our worst evil."

First printing. Printed in U.S.A.

Published simultaneously in Canada.
School and library distribution by Silver Burdett
Company, Morristown, New Jersey 07960.

TIME-LIFE is a trademark of Time Warner Inc.
U.S.A.

**Library of Congress Cataloging in
Publication Data**
Wolf Packs / by the editors of Time-Life Books.
  p.   cm. — (The Third Reich)
  Bibliography: p.
  Includes index.
  ISBN 0-8094-6975-8
  ISBN 0-8094-6976-6 (lib. bdg.)
  1. World War, 1939-1945—Naval operations—
Submarine. 2. World War, 1939-1945—Naval
operations, German. I. Time-Life Books.
II. Series.
D781.W6 1989   940.54'51'0943—dc20   89-4559

This volume is one of a series that chronicles the
rise and eventual fall of Nazi Germany. Other books
in the series include:
The SS
Fists of Steel
Storming to Power
The New Order
The Reach for Empire
Lightning War

General Consultants

Col. John R. Elting, USA (Ret.), former asso-
ciate professor at West Point, has written or
edited some twenty books, including *Swords
around a Throne, The Superstrategists,* and
American Army Life, as well as *Battles for
Scandinavia* in the Time-Life Books World
War II series. He was chief consultant to the
Time-Life series, The Civil War.

Timothy Patrick Mulligan is an archivist and
editor for the National Archives in Washington, D.C., specializing in American and captured German World War II military records.
He holds a Ph.D. in diplomatic history from
the University of Maryland and has published his dissertation, *The Politics of Illu-
sion and Empire: German Occupation Policy
in the Soviet Union, 1942-1943.* In addition,
he has published articles on U-boat warfare
and compiled a catalog of U-boat war diaries
held on microfilm by the National Archives.

Contents

A German submarine on combat patrol rides out rough weather in the North Atlantic.

Crew members on bridge watch scan the horizon for enemy ships and planes.

An unsuspecting freighter is caught in the cross hairs of a submerged U-boat's attack periscope.

Victim of a German torpedo, a British ship carrying munitions erupts with a mighty explosion.

Birth of the "U-boat Peril"

Lean and intense, U-boat chief Karl Dönitz *(far right)* stands next to Grand Admiral Erich Raeder on the conning tower of a new German submarine in October 1939. The two officers disagreed on the importance and role of U-boats in the war just begun.

aptain Karl Dönitz, commanding officer of Germany's submarine fleet, faced the prospect of a war he felt ill equipped to fight. On September 1, 1939, Adolf Hitler, without warning, had invaded Poland. The invasion itself posed no problem for Dönitz, who was ready to support it. He had deployed twenty-four coastal U-boats in the Baltic and North seas to confront the tiny Polish navy and the ships of any Polish ally, such as France, that might sail to the country's assistance. What haunted Dönitz was the wider war that the incursion might spawn. For years, and with increasing stridency in recent months, Dönitz had insisted that neither his U-boat fleet nor the German navy was prepared to take on the British navy, the mightiest in the world. Germany had only two battleships to Britain's fifteen, and no aircraft carriers to England's six. The Royal Navy possessed eight times as many cruisers and five times as many destroyers and torpedo boats as the German navy. The Reich could not hope to successfully engage Britain on the high seas. True, the island nation was vulnerable to disruption of the merchant shipping it depended on for survival. But for that major task, Dönitz maintained, he would need not only the 56 submarines that were under his command in the late summer of 1939, but at least 300.

When he had made his case to the navy's commander in chief, Erich Raeder, during U-boat exercises in the Baltic in July, the admiral had reassured him that the conflict with Poland would not be allowed to spread. Hitler had things well in hand, Raeder had asserted. Like Dönitz, he passionately opposed embroiling Germany in another two-front war, but the Führer himself had vowed to him that the Reich would not fight Britain, and Raeder believed him. He even repeated the promise in a speech to his officers on July 22: "Do not believe that the Führer would lead us into such a desperate situation," he stated.

Hitler had already astonished his military commanders, along with observers in the rest of the world, by remilitarizing the Rhineland and occupying the countries of Austria and Czechoslovakia. It now seemed reasonable to think that he could get away with crushing Poland. On the day

of Raeder's speech, Dönitz left his beloved U-boat command for what was supposed to be six weeks of rest and recuperation after four years of ceaseless labor to create a powerful undersea fleet. But he was recalled on August 15 as the Third Reich mobilized.

Dönitz had two command posts for his fleet, one aboard ship at Kiel, Germany's primary port on the Baltic, and another in a barracks in Wilhelmshaven, on the North Sea. Harboring the increasingly forlorn hope that war would be confined to the Baltic, he remained at Kiel until the end of August. On August 31, he moved to Wilhelmshaven, although he still refused to dismiss the possibility that the British would stand aside and let Poland fall. At half past six that evening, Dönitz sent a message to all U-boats: "No attacks against English forces except in self-defense or by special order. Attitude of Western powers still uncertain."

When the Germans struck the next morning, London hesitated and agonized. Then, after forty-eight hours of excruciating tension, Great Britain declared war. The British Admiralty flashed a terse, uncoded signal to

Admiral Raeder raises the baton symbolic of his rank, and Captain Dönitz offers a hand salute as the U-51, its crew arrayed smartly on deck, passes in review during prewar exercises on the Baltic Sea.

all its ships at sea: "Total Germany." Minutes later, a copy of the intercepted message was handed to Dönitz. Stunned by its implications, he paced blindly up and down in his situation room, muttering, "My God! So it's war against England again!" When he realized that his subordinates were staring at him, he left the room. Half an hour later, he returned, once more the stern commander, ready to face the conflict that he believed had come too soon. "We know our enemy," he told his men firmly. "Today we have the weapon"—by that he meant the U-boat fleet—"and leaders who can face up to this enemy. The war will last a long time, but if each of us does his duty, we will win. Now to your tasks!"

Grand Admiral Raeder was also deeply upset by England's entry into the war on September 3. He heard the news that afternoon, while presiding over a staff meeting. Raeder, too, left the room to conceal his despair from subordinates and to write a bitter memorandum for the record. If he had received the five years of shipbuilding that Hitler had promised, Raeder wrote, the navy would have been ready to confront the British fleet and cut off supplies to the British Isles—ready to impose, as he put it, the "final solution to the English question." Instead, Raeder wrote, the only course left to the German navy was to show "that it understands how to die with honor." On that Sunday afternoon, the submariners of the German fleet received a brisk order from their dejected commanders. "Commence hostilities against Britain forthwith," it read. And on the next afternoon, as if in confirmation of Dönitz's bleak expectations, the air over Wilhelmshaven vibrated with the drone of British bombers and shuddered with the concussion of British bombs.

Despite his pessimism, Dönitz and his seemingly inadequate fleet of submarines were about to become the weapon the leaders of the United Kingdom and its allies feared most. Armor and infantry combined in panzer divisions would crush Europe and threaten Britain with invasion, and the Luftwaffe would pound London from the air, but Dönitz's lone raiders and so-called wolf packs would come closest to strangling that defiant nation. German U-boats would sink 14 million tons of Allied and neutral shipping, much of it intended to supply Britain with the matériel its military needed to fight and the food its people required to survive. "The only thing that ever really frightened me during the war," Winston Churchill would write years later, "was the U-boat peril."

A grim Karl Dönitz, released from the British internment camp where he had spent the last months of World War I, reported for duty in July of 1919 to the German navy station at Kiel. Though not physically imposing—Dönitz was of average height and very lean—his hawklike features and ramrod bearing made him seem taller. His greeting from Lieut. Commander Otto Schultze, a former commanding officer who was now adjutant of the navy, was a blunt question. "Are you going to stay with us, Dönitz?"

That he was even asked was an honor of sorts; the Treaty of Versailles permitted the postwar German navy a mere 1,500 officers, and only the best were being invited to stay on. Dönitz had built a fine record since entering the navy in 1910, when he was eighteen years old. Although he had come from a middle-class family characterized by no particular tradition of military service, he had adopted the stern outlook and rigorous discipline of the much-admired Prussian officer corps. His attitude, leavened by a lively mind and a concern for the welfare of subordinates that was not always found in true Junkers, was warmly received in the navy and earned Dönitz steady advancement.

Dönitz began the Great War as a flight observer in the naval air arm, became the commander of a seaplane squadron, and in 1916 transferred to submarines. He received command of his own boat in 1918, and his reputation survived the incident that resulted in his capture and internment by the British. Off the south coast of Sicily on October 4, 1918, Dönitz's submerged craft was stricken by mechanical failures. He brought it to the surface in the middle of a fleet of enemy warships. He and his men had to abandon ship. The British plucked him from the sea, and he spent several months in prison before being repatriated.

In 1919, however, Dönitz needed assurances before deciding whether to stay on in the postwar navy. He responded to the adjutant's question with one of his own. "Do you think we shall have U-boats again?" he asked.

As Dönitz well knew, the Treaty of Versailles permitted only a tiny German navy with a few dozen surface ships—no U-boats and no aircraft. But he also realized that nothing in Germany was as it appeared. Key figures in government and the military were already planning ways to evade the rearmament strictures of Versailles and rebuild Germany's armed forces. Thus Schultze had a ready answer for Dönitz. "Things won't always be like this," he said. "Within a couple of years or so, I hope we shall once again have U-boats."

With that encouragement, Dönitz promptly signed on to assist Schultze in selecting the men who would rebuild the navy. The process was interrupted in March 1920, when several high-ranking naval officers joined a right-wing putsch that briefly installed a new government in Berlin headed by an inconspicuous civil servant named Wolfgang Kapp. The Kapp regime lasted only five days, and Dönitz skillfully navigated around the perilous situation. Somehow, he gained command of a torpedo boat with a loyal crew and sailed away from Kiel, returning only after the trouble was

Mutinous sailors—joined by a few disgruntled soldiers—cluster around a captured armored car in the courtyard of the royal palace in Berlin in November 1918. Designated the People's Marine Division, the sailors were part of the sporadic socialist uprisings that rocked Germany for months after the abdication of Kaiser Wilhelm II.

over. The Weimar government punished a few of the rebellious officers, and the rest returned to the business of rearming. Dönitz was assigned command of a torpedo boat based in the Baltic port of Swinemünde.

For nearly fifteen years, that would be as close as Dönitz would get to a U-boat. Schultze had greatly underestimated the time that would be required to clandestinely rebuild a submarine fleet. In fact, the entire navy had difficulty re-creating itself beyond the prying eyes of the Allied treaty inspectors. The army could stash its illicit weapons in a cave somewhere, and the air force could hide a few airplanes in remote Russian hangars, but where could the navy build a battleship or a submarine in secret? Nevertheless, preparations went forward. Secret funds were established, reliable people were recruited for shadow organizations, and forbidden planning took place in obscure offices. Much of the unaccounted money went to a concern in the Netherlands known as the Dutch Submarine-Development Bureau, where German naval engineers and officers in civilian clothes designed and helped build submarines for sale to various countries. Before delivery, German crews took the boats on unusually long and thorough shakedown cruises.

In the meantime, Dönitz concentrated on his own career. He pushed himself and his torpedo-boat crews hard, planning and conducting exercises as though war were imminent. He invented and tried out new tactics and techniques, and he criticized the results harshly. Dönitz spared neither himself nor his men, but he always shared their hardships and took pains to cultivate an atmosphere of fellowship. An evaluation written by his commanding officer in 1921 praised his "exemplary service outlook and fullest devotion to duty."

After three years on torpedo boats, Dönitz was transferred in 1923 to staff duty in Kiel to advise on submarine-hunting methods and depth-charge development. There he met the navy's rising stars, including Erich Raeder, then a rear admiral, and Wilhelm Canaris, who would become head of the *Abwehr*, the intelligence service of the High Command of the Armed Forces. He shared with such men not only devotion to the German navy, but a profound hatred of communism, a deep sense of shame at the outcome of World War I, a distaste for the impotent Weimar government, and— eventually—a growing regard for the Nazi party.

These like-minded men saw in Dönitz a surpassingly valuable leader for the future navy. "Clever, industrious, ambitious officer," Raeder noted enthusiastically in 1924. "Excellently gifted for his post, above average, tough and brisk officer," wrote his commanding officer in 1929, shortly after Dönitz had been promoted to lieutenant commander and placed in charge of three torpedo boats.

Dönitz's promise was further recognized when he received a travel grant awarded each year to an outstanding officer. He left Germany in February of 1933, just as Hitler grasped the reins of power, for a leisurely five-month tour of the Far East. Then, after a year of staff work, during which he was made a commander, and a visit to Britain in the summer of 1934, he took command of the light cruiser *Emden* and left in November for a lengthy cruise to African and Indian waters.

Germany still did not have a U-boat to its name. The secret design work had continued in Holland, Finland, and—after 1926—an office hidden in the city of Berlin. In 1932, the High Command of the Navy (OKM) had completed its plan for the resumption of U-boat construction, and in 1933 had begun training crews. By the fall of 1934, enough parts to assemble ten submarines had been fabricated in Spain, the Netherlands, and Finland, then shipped to Kiel for storage.

Much happened in Germany before Dönitz returned home in June of 1935. In March, Hitler repudiated the disarmament clauses of the Versailles treaty and proclaimed Germany to be a sovereign nation once again. When the victors of World War I did nothing to enforce the treaty except register a protest, the German government unveiled its growing armories. Hermann Göring announced the existence of the Luftwaffe, which Hitler boasted was the equal of the Royal Air Force. The Führer also proclaimed the conscription of young men for an army of thirty-six divisions.

Then Hitler scored a diplomatic coup that invigorated German naval rearmament. In June, he announced a treaty with Britain that limited the size of Germany's navy to 35 percent that of the British fleet. While the treaty formula seemed to freeze Germany in a permanently inferior position on the seas, it actually gave the tiny navy license to build furiously. The agreement also won Britain's tacit acceptance of the existence of German armed forces, despite the Versailles rules. And it cracked the Stresa Front, a pact uniting Britain, France, and Italy against German aggression.

The naval treaty represented an important step in Hitler's grand scheme to develop a special relationship with Britain that would prevent the powerful country from interfering with his future conquests in eastern Europe. Under the terms of the treaty, submarines were a special case; Germany was permitted an undersea force 45 percent as large as the British, a concession that did not alarm British naval strategists. The Royal Navy felt little need for submarines and possessed only about fifty of them. Moreover, near the end of World War I, Great Britain had developed a submarine-locating device called asdic (an acronym for the Allied Submarine Detection Investigation Committee, which supervised its development). This device, called sonar by American naval personnel, projected a beam of sound underwater and interpreted any echoes returning from objects beneath the waves. Under the right conditions, asdic could determine the range and bearing of a submerged submarine several thousand yards away. British strategists believed that asdic would neutralize any submarine threat: According to one admiralty paper, "The U-boat will never again be capable of confronting us with the problem with which we found ourselves faced in 1917."

Just as the Royal Navy overestimated its defensive capabilities, it underestimated Germany's aggressiveness. A complacent admiralty analysis of the naval agreement suggested that the best way to ensure moderation on the part of the Germans was to give them what they wanted. The attitude would delight Hitler and take Britain to the brink of destruction. The Führer told Raeder that June 18, 1935, when the agreement was signed, was the happiest day of his life.

In fact, by that day, Hitler's first U-boat had been launched; ten days later, it was formally commissioned the U-1. By September 28, nine more boats

had slid down the ways at Kiel to form a flotilla that was placed under the command of Karl Dönitz, newly promoted to full captain. "I had received neither orders, instructions, nor guidance," Dönitz recalled of his appointment, but he considered the neglect an advantage. His independent status gave him a chance to apply unfettered everything he had learned in submarines during the Great War and in torpedo boats afterward. "Body and soul," he wrote later, "I was once more a submariner."

Dönitz's first objective was to infect his officers and men with his enthusiasm for this unorthodox weapon. He scoffed at the idea that the development of asdic had rendered the U-boat obsolete, although no one really knew how the British device would perform in combat. The U-boat school had been teaching German submariners to launch their torpedoes from almost two miles away to avoid detection by asdic; Dönitz pronounced this nonsense and mandated a firing range of 600 yards. To instill confidence in his men, he conducted grueling exercises designed to reproduce the rigors of combat as exactly as possible.

Dönitz required each boat's crew to successfully complete sixty-six surface and sixty-six underwater exercises before it practiced actually

A signalman wigwags from the conning tower of the U-1, the Third Reich's first submarine, as it glides through a calm sea off Kiel in June 1935. Built in secret to circumvent the strictures of the Versailles treaty, the 254-ton boat was considered too small to operate beyond coastal waters.

firing a torpedo. As often as not, Dönitz could be found at the shoulder of one of his U-boat commanders, guiding the hand of a control-room engineer, or working out a problem in the engine room. During an exercise in 1936, a boat making an emergency deep dive sprang a leak and was nearly lost. Alarmed, the naval high command henceforth limited practice dives to 150 feet, much to Dönitz's disgust. He believed that the safety limit deprived his crews of valuable experience. As he would eventually learn, the proscription also postponed the discovery of a serious flaw in the U-boats themselves. The valve that kept water out of the diesel engines' exhaust lines was poorly designed and leaked during deep dives. The defect may have caused the loss of several boats in combat before it was exposed. "For the lessons that one fails to learn in peace," Dönitz said, "one pays a high price in war."

"The U-boat is wholly and essentially an attack weapon," he wrote in 1935, and he preached this doctrine relentlessly. In addition to the traditional submerged attacks on enemy ships during the day, Dönitz initiated surface attacks at night. Asdic could not find U-boats on the surface, and in the darkness, the submarines' low profiles made them extremely difficult to see, let alone hit. They could get close to the enemy and deliver point-blank torpedo attacks.

After a year of intense training, Dönitz and his men received the first of a new type of U-boat. Their old boats were Type IIs, which displaced 279 tons, possessed three bow torpedo tubes, reached a top speed when surfaced of thirteen knots, and had a range of about 1,800 miles at twelve knots. Dönitz deemed this craft a "very simple and successful vessel, but very small." The new submarines, designated Type VII after several abortive starts, were 761-ton boats with four torpedo tubes in the bow and one in the stern, a surface speed of seventeen knots, and a range of more than 6,000 miles at twelve knots, soon increased to almost 9,000 miles. This Dönitz pronounced an "excellent type."

Now in overall command as *Führer der U-Boote*, Dönitz evolved increasingly unorthodox tactics. For him, the lessons of World War I were clear: The practice of sending U-boats out alone to attack any ships that happened into view had worked well only until the enemy adopted convoys. Then the chances were slight that a lone boat would even find a convoy. When it did, the convoy's defenses greatly reduced the likelihood of a successful U-boat attack.

Sometime in 1936, Dönitz began experimenting with an approach that was first suggested in 1917 but never used in battle. He deployed a group of U-boats in a broad arc across a probable convoy route, thus increasing the chances that one of the boats would spot a procession of enemy ships.

When it did, it would track the convoy while summoning the nearby U-boats by radio. Then the Germans would attack in strength from the flanks and rear and, if possible, while operating on the surface at night. These methods would come to be known—in a metaphor that pleased Nazi propagandists—as wolf-pack tactics.

Like most innovations, however, this one failed to appeal to the staff of the naval high command. Naval planners, responsible for formulating global strategy, envisioned U-boats functioning in the next war as they had in the last—alone and at long range. Thus the OKM foresaw the construction of gargantuan U-cruisers of 2,000 tons' displacement, equipped with heavy guns for surface artillery duels and capable of global operations. Dönitz, the natural champion of the wolf-pack tactics, wanted a large U-boat fleet, not a few supersize behemoths. In his view, building large boats wasted resources. The navy could build several type-VII boats for the time, effort, and expense required to build a single U-cruiser.

Dönitz refused to accept his superiors' judgment, and during 1937 his disagreement with them, as he put it, "became increasingly acute." He applied to the struggle all the logic and forcefulness he could bring to bear, exerting an influence far beyond his relatively modest rank. The result was not victory, but stalemate; Raeder could not decide what to do, and the shipyards that had delivered twenty-one U-boats in 1936 produced only one in 1937. That fall, Dönitz conducted the first large-scale exercises designed to test the new wolf-pack tactics and confirmed, at least to his satisfaction, that they worked admirably. He redoubled his efforts to change the high command's thinking.

At the time, Germany's entire naval shipbuilding program was in trouble. The army, the Luftwaffe, and the builders of the defensive West Wall had claimed most of the available steel, and the navy suffered chronic shortages. Raeder had complained about the shortfall for a year, and on October 25, 1937, he delivered a threat; either he received more steel or he would drastically cut the building program in order to finish at least a few ships "in a conceivable time."

Moreover, the planners faced a crucial theoretical question: What kind of war should the navy prepare to fight? The strategists had foreseen a war against Poland and possibly France, which implied battle in the Baltic, the North Sea, and the Mediterranean. But if war with Great Britain could not be avoided, German ships would have to fight an immensely more powerful fleet in waters both near and far. Raeder needed not only steel, but a clear-cut policy for using it.

The future came more clearly into focus for Raeder and his fellow military commanders later that autumn. At a meeting on November 5, the

The nine principal submarine types built in Germany beginning in 1934 are shown right. They were a mixed b of excellent and inferior boa The early Type I was a failure It handled poorly, and or two were commissioned. T Type IIs were better, agile a reliable, but small. After 19 they were used mainly training in the Baltic.

The Type VIIs, especia the improved "C" versions 1938, were efficient, fast, a maneuverable fighting m chines. More than 660 we built, over half of the Reicl total production. The type boats had greater range a armament than the VIIs a sank more tonnage per bo than any other model.

Two U-boats served as su ply vessels, the Type X, a co verted minelayer, and th Type XIV, the 1,688-ton Milc kuh, or milk cow, which ca ried as much as 432 tons extra fuel for combat U-boa

Improved antisubmari technology demanded boats that could stay su merged longer. The expe mental Type XVII was fa underwater but too small carry sufficient armamen The Types XXI and XXIII, bo electric boats, combine speed and fighting ability ar could stay under for days. B they came so late that on one of the large, powerful XX —and none of the XXIIIs ever saw an enemy ship.

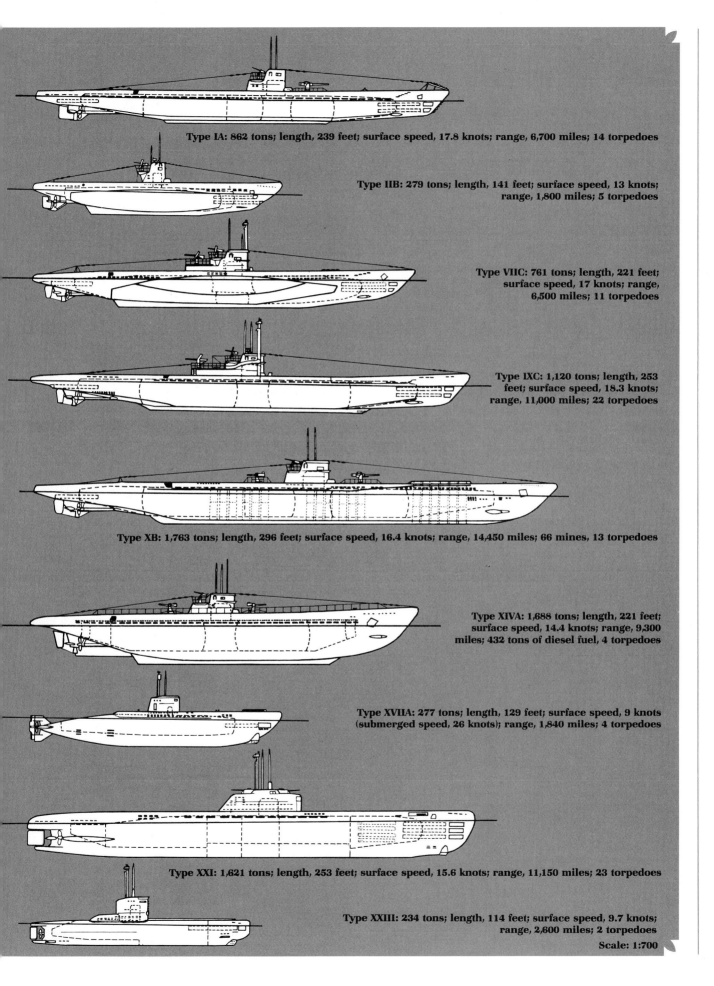

Type IA: 862 tons; length, 239 feet; surface speed, 17.8 knots; range, 6,700 miles; 14 torpedoes

Type IIB: 279 tons; length, 141 feet; surface speed, 13 knots; range, 1,800 miles; 5 torpedoes

Type VIIC: 761 tons; length, 221 feet; surface speed, 17 knots; range, 6,500 miles; 11 torpedoes

Type IXC: 1,120 tons; length, 253 feet; surface speed, 18.3 knots; range, 11,000 miles; 22 torpedoes

Type XB: 1,763 tons; length, 296 feet; surface speed, 16.4 knots; range, 14,450 miles; 66 mines, 13 torpedoes

Type XIVA: 1,688 tons; length, 221 feet; surface speed, 14.4 knots; range, 9,300 miles; 432 tons of diesel fuel, 4 torpedoes

Type XVIIA: 277 tons; length, 129 feet; surface speed, 9 knots (submerged speed, 26 knots); range, 1,840 miles; 4 torpedoes

Type XXI: 1,621 tons; length, 253 feet; surface speed, 15.6 knots; range, 11,150 miles; 23 torpedoes

Type XXIII: 234 tons; length, 114 feet; surface speed, 9.7 knots; range, 2,600 miles; 2 torpedoes

Scale: 1:700

23

A roughly half-size replica of the U-9 is displayed between antiaircraft guns and the huge figure of a soldier at a 1937 exhibition in Berlin. Hitler used the show to let the world know of Germany's swift rearmament.

Führer recognized the possibility of war with Britain, but only if a general war developed and certainly not before 1943. Meanwhile, Raeder would have his steel, and he must build ships quickly. Still, the navy could not decide on a building program. Remarkably, yet another year passed—a year in which Hitler risked war by annexing nearby Austria and then announced the even more dangerous intention of dismantling Czechoslovakia—before the high command even examined the requirements of naval warfare against Great Britain.

Eventually, the planners presented Hitler with two options. The navy could prepare quickly for a war against Britain's vital supply lines by building a sizable fleet of U-boats and pocket battleships. Or it could take ten years to complete a fleet so large and diverse that it could both attack merchant shipping and confront the formidable Royal Navy. Hitler chose the grandiose plan, making one change; he directed that the armada be completed in six years instead of ten. He ordered a fleet that, if built, would burn more oil than all of Germany consumed in 1938.

Dönitz was dismayed. He found it inconceivable that Britain would stand by while a potential enemy built such a massive fleet. In his view, there was only enough time left before war broke out to build a large fleet of medium-size U-boats. He calculated that at least 100 submarines would be needed on patrol in the Atlantic Ocean to put an economic stranglehold on Great Britain. In truth, this meant a fleet of 300, since two-thirds of the vessels would always be either in port for resupply and repair or in transit. Such a building program would obviously be impossible, he said in early 1939, for "the next few years."

By that time, only months remained. In late March, Hitler secretly told his commanders to be ready to invade Poland by September 1. And on April 26, he confounded his policy of lulling Britain by publicly repudiating the Anglo-German Naval Agreement of 1935. Dönitz's alarm, which Raeder cautiously relayed to the Führer, had no effect. Hitler continued to assure the navy it would not have to fight the British fleet, virtually to the day the signal "Total Germany" flashed from London.

While the invasion of Poland by land and air erupted with the furious thunder of bombs and artillery, the sea war began quietly and hesitantly. To avoid undue provocation of Britain and France, Dönitz's U-boat captains received strict orders to adhere to international maritime law. According

Thirteen boats of the Weddigen Flotilla, the beginning of Hitler's U-boat fleet, lie alongside their tender at Kiel in 1937. The flotilla was named for Otto Weddigen, a World War I U-boat commander who had sunk three British cruisers in one day.

Photographed by a camera mounted on the bow, the U-27 sends up a cascade of sea spray while moving on the surface. Once the war began, the number on the conning tower was painted out for security's sake.

to the so-called Prize Ordinance, attacks on passenger liners were prohibited. A submarine interdicting a merchant ship was required to surface, challenge and halt the transport, and determine whether it carried military contraband. If so, the submarine had a right to seize the ship or sink it, but only after providing for the safety of the crew.

The Germans sought to avoid the pattern they had set during the First World War. Germany had desperately wanted to keep the United States out of the conflict, but in the spring of 1915, its U-boat fleet committed a major blunder by torpedoing passenger liners that happened to be carrying Americans. Among the victimized ships was the *Lusitania*, which was sent to the bottom of the ocean by the U-20 with a loss of 1,198 lives, including 128 American citizens. The United States joined an international chorus of outrage at the depredations of the U-boats, and an embarrassed German navy abandoned its policy of unlimited submarine warfare and began observing international law. But it was too late. The U-boat attacks had helped to harden American public opinion against Germany and paved the way for a declaration of war.

Remarkably, the same mistakes marked the beginning of the U-boat war in 1939. The first ship sunk by a German submarine, on the day Great Britain declared war, was an unarmed British passenger ship, the *Athenia*. After night had fallen on September 3, the U-30 spotted the *Athenia*, outward-bound in the North Atlantic, running with lights extinguished and following a zigzag course. The captain of the U-boat concluded that the vessel was a troopship. Without observing any of the protocols, he torpedoed the *Athenia* and left its 1,103 passengers (including about 300 Americans) to their fate. The death toll was 128.

The German government denied any role in the sinking and, in fact, did not learn the details until the U-30 returned to its base at the end of September. The Germans even accused Winston Churchill, who had just been named first lord of the admiralty, of arranging the disaster to discredit the Reich. Nevertheless, Hitler was furious over the incident. He wasted no time in clamping additional restrictions on the U-boats: no further attacks on passenger liners, no attacks whatever on French shipping.

Dönitz's frustration grew. With only twenty-two widely dispersed boats roaming the Atlantic, he had no chance to apply his wolf-pack tactics. Soon the cycle of refitting and resupply drastically reduced even this small force. Moreover, the strictures of international law put the U-boats at a grave disadvantage. A submarine forced to surface to engage an enemy exposed itself to the concealed guns of armed merchant ships—the U-38 was nearly sunk when a cargo vessel opened fire on September 6—and risked being seen and attacked by patrolling aircraft.

And from the outset, mechanical failures haunted the U-boat offensive. Dönitz lost his first boat on September 14, when the U-39 attacked the British aircraft carrier *Ark Royal*. The submarine's torpedoes detonated too soon, attracting British destroyers, which attacked and sank the German craft. Worse, there was no building program to replace lost U-boats, let alone expand the fleet to its required strength. In desperation, Dönitz regretfully volunteered to leave his command to take charge of development and construction, but he was told to stay where he was.

Dönitz took what comfort he could from occasional successes. On September 17, the U-29 managed to sink the British aircraft carrier *Courageous* with 519 personnel aboard. The loss forced Britain to withdraw the rest of its carriers from the Atlantic. As Dönitz boasted, the retreat confirmed that "British countermeasures are not as effective as they maintain."

Meanwhile, Dönitz chipped away at the shackles of the Prize Ordinance. Merchant vessels that were challenged by U-boats had adopted the practice of transmitting the letters "SSS"—meaning "attacked by submarine"—and their position. Dönitz correctly assumed the signal was an appeal for help from British air and sea patrols. He interpreted this as participation by the merchant ship in a military operation, an action that voided the requirements of the Prize Ordinance. On September 23, Hitler agreed to Dönitz's request for permission to attack any ship that broadcast the signal after it was challenged.

Four days later, the Polish capital fell, and for the first time in the war, Hitler turned his attention from the enthralling performance of his panzers and dive bombers to the activities of his navy. A number of U-boats were coming home for fuel, supplies, and torpedoes after completing their first cruises in the Atlantic Ocean, and Hitler went to Dönitz's headquarters at Wilhelmshaven to see them.

Dönitz used the occasion to deliver an impassioned sermon to Hitler on the worthiness of his fleet and the need to expand it. His boats had already sunk 135,000 tons of enemy shipping and discredited the vaunted British submarine defenses. U-boats could be even more effective than they had been during the previous war, he said, because their radio communications had been vastly improved and their new electric torpedoes left no telltale wakes. A German fleet of 300 U-boats using wolf-pack tactics, Dönitz asserted to the Führer, would be a "means of inflicting decisive damage on England at its weakest point."

Understandably, Dönitz did not dwell upon the more troubling aspects of his first month of war. The auspicious beginning had been made with twenty-two boats at sea; henceforth, all but about fifteen would be either in port or in transit. Two submarines had been lost. In addition, a troubling

A lifeboat from the freighter *City of Flint* transfers two wounded passengers from the torpedoed British liner *Athenia* to an American cutter that stood by to help. Bound for the United States, the *Athenia* had been carrying civilians trying to escape the war raging in Europe.

number of torpedoes had either missed or misfired. Nevertheless, Hitler went away from the meeting impressed. On September 30, Dönitz was promoted to rear admiral. Two weeks later, the Führer had even more reason to admire his U-boat commander.

On the moonless night of October 13, 1939, Lieut. Commander Günther Prien brought the U-47 to the surface just outside Scapa Flow, a broad harbor enclosed by the Orkney Islands and the main base of the British Home Fleet. The various channels into the harbor were either heavily patrolled or blocked by sunken ships and steel netting. Admiral Dönitz had studied aerial photographs of the harbor, however, and discovered that a fifty-five-foot gap separated two of the hulks blocking the eastern entrance past Lamb Holm Island, room for a well-handled U-boat to slip through. Dönitz had sent his best commander to explore the possibility of striking a devastating blow against Britain.

After completing their first combat patrol, all U-boat personnel qualified to wear this decoration, the Submarine War Badge.

As Prien clambered through the hatch to the conning tower, he expected to find the darkness he craved. Instead, he was dismayed to see a sky ablaze with a brilliant display of northern lights. Nevertheless, he pressed on. As the submarine approached the gap between the blockships, swept forward by the fierce tide that was surging into the Flow, Prien suddenly spotted disaster looming. Strung between the blockships lay a line twelve inches thick and several cables as thick as six inches. He could clearly see the white water swirling around the cables where they sloped from the hulks and angled beneath the surface. The current was too strong to turn back or reverse. Prien steered for the center of the gap, where the cables should be deepest, hoping that his vessel would scrape over them.

As the U-boat's keel struck and then began to slide over the cables, the creaking moan of metal against metal reverberated through the hull and sent a chill of fear through the forty members of the crew, who suspected that the sub had hit a mine mooring and that they would be blown to bits at any moment. Instead, the vessel passed safely over the line and cables and the noise stopped. But the trouble did not. The contact had slued the submarine to starboard. With a bump, it went aground and held fast.

In a picture taken from an escort destroyer, the aircraft carrier *Courageous* heels over after being hit twice by torpedoes off the Irish coast on September 17, 1939. The ship's loss was the first major setback for the Royal Navy in the war at sea.

Prien tried maneuvering the boat off with combinations of rudder and engine, all to no avail. If the craft was still stuck at dawn, it would belong to the British, along with its crew. To lighten the craft, Prien ordered the water expelled from the diving tanks, which had been partially flooded to make the submarine heavier and hence lower its silhouette. To the relief of all, the U-47 immediately floated free. Prien fought the current for control, finally steadied his boat, and turned its bow to the west, into the dark openness of Scapa Flow.

Prien scoured the surface with his night binoculars, expecting to spy the British fleet looming on the horizon. To his amazement, there was only empty water. He rode westward for three and a half miles, searching around the compass with the glasses, and saw not a single vessel. A terrible mistake had been made—the British Home Fleet was not in Scapa Flow. Growing more desperate by the minute, Prien retraced his course for a time and then turned north to probe the northeast corner of the harbor, the only area he had not searched. Finally, a long dark shadow emerged on the surface of the Flow. As he grew closer, he could make out against the sky the unmistakable superstructure of a British battleship, the *Royal Oak*. About a mile beyond that vessel, partially obscured by its hull, lay another

British warship. Prien thought that both were battleships; in fact, the other was a seaplane tender, HMS *Pegasus*.

Shortly after midnight, Prien attacked. He ordered three torpedoes fired in a fan pattern, one aimed at the bow of the distant enemy vessel and two at the hull of the nearer, looming ship. As each projectile shot from its tube, the submarine bounced. The German crewmen waited in tense silence for the sound of explosions.

One of the torpedoes struck the *Royal Oak* in the bow and opened a gaping hole near the keel. The blow was enough to be fatal, but the explosion was muffled throughout most of the ship and no alarm was sounded. On board the U-47, Prien thought that one of the torpedoes had hit the distant ship and the other two had missed. Neither seemed to be in any difficulty, so Prien turned his stern to the targets and fired his aft torpedo, apparently missing again. Then he withdrew southward while the crew reloaded all five tubes.

When all was ready, eighteen minutes later, he fired again. This time, the submarine commander got three solid hits, one of which ignited the *Royal Oak*'s magazine. A stupendous explosion hurled a cascade of scrap metal into the harbor. The great ship immediately heeled drunkenly to starboard and then rolled over. Most of the 1,200 crewmen were trapped belowdecks with little chance of escape. In less than half an hour after the first torpedo had struck, the battleship turned turtle and sank with the loss of 833 men. The *Pegasus* escaped unharmed.

Prien and his crew heard the explosions clearly. The fatal blow had been dealt; it was time to make a getaway. Since the tide was swiftly ebbing, Prien chose a deeper but narrower passage on the south side of the blockships. Fortunately for him, no cables spanned the exit. Borne by the fierce outflow, the German boat swept between an island and a sunken hulk with inches of beam room to spare. Two hours after entering Scapa Flow, the U-47 reached the safety of the North Sea.

There was more to the victory. Dönitz had calculated that if Prien made good his attack, the British fleet would disperse to other anchorages until Scapa Flow could be made more secure. Prior to the mission, Dönitz had ordered his submarines to lay mines in the three most likely refuges—Scotland's Loch Ewe, Firth of Forth, and Firth of Clyde. Dönitz's hunch was partially correct, but the British acted sooner than he anticipated. By October 10, as Prien made his way toward his target, most of the British fleet had abandoned Scapa Flow, fearing indeed that the haven was not safe from a submarine attack. Only the *Royal Oak*, the *Pegasus*, and a few auxiliary vessels remained. The other warships dispersed—directly into Dönitz's traps. German mines severely damaged a new British cruiser in

Daring Thrust into a Hostile Anchorage

The astonishing attack on the Royal Navy's supposedly impregnable anchorage at Scapa Flow began much like any early U-boat foray into the North Sea. Taking his U-47 out of the submarine lair at Kiel on October 8, 1939, Günther Prien sailed through the Kiel Canal and northwestward toward the tip of Scotland (*right*).

By October 13, the U-47 lay submerged off the Orkney Islands. Prien surfaced at nightfall and slipped silently into Kirk Sound, one of the narrow channels leading to the nearly landlocked anchorage. He then wriggled through a tiny gap between two sunken blockships (*map, inset*), and, a few minutes after midnight, moved across the dark waters of Scapa Flow itself.

To his disgust, Prien found those waters empty. The British Home Fleet was gone, moved to another anchorage. But edging northward, Prien saw a huge, shadowy shape: the battleship *Royal Oak*, left behind for repairs. His first torpedo salvo produced no visible result, so Prien, circling while he reloaded, attacked again. This time, three torpedoes hit home, nearly tearing the 29,000-ton battleship apart and killing 833 members of its crew.

An exultant Prien quickly headed back for Kirk Sound, squeezing through another perilously tight gap, then sped across the North Sea for Wilhelmshaven—where he and his crew received a hero's welcome (*next pages*).

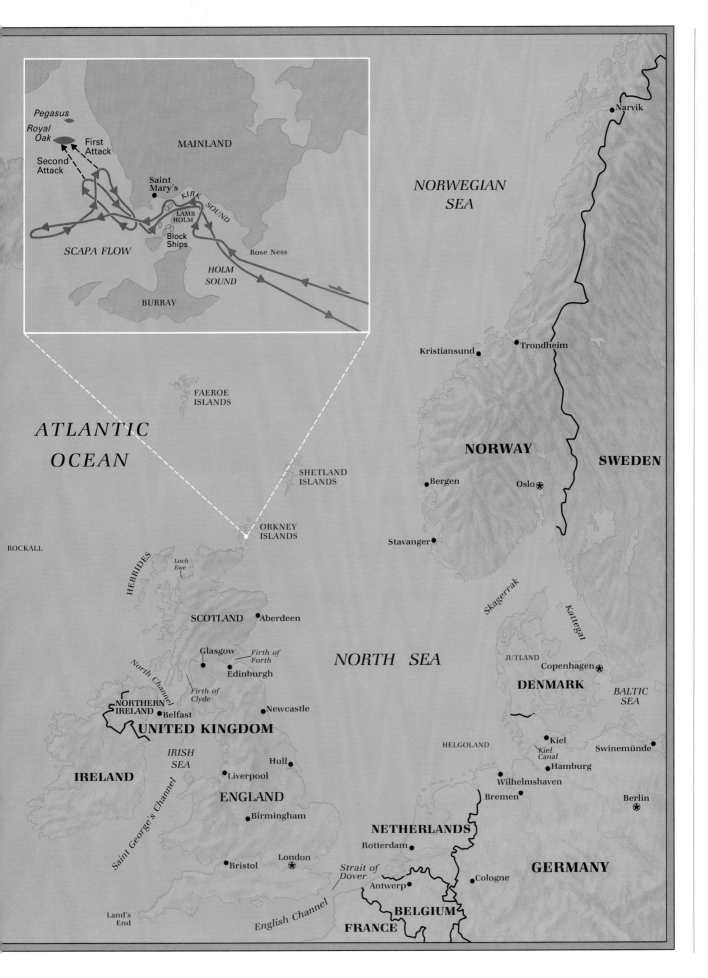

Pegasus

Royal Oak

First Attack

Second Attack

MAINLAND

Saint Mary's

KIRK SOUND

LAMB HOLM

Block Ships

SCAPA FLOW

Rose Ness

HOLM SOUND

BURRAY

ATLANTIC OCEAN

FAEROE ISLANDS

NORWEGIAN SEA

Narvik

Kristiansund

Trondheim

SHETLAND ISLANDS

NORWAY

SWEDEN

Bergen

Oslo ✪

ROCKALL

ORKNEY ISLANDS

Stavanger

HEBRIDES

Loch Ewe

Skagerrak

Kattegat

SCOTLAND

Aberdeen

NORTH SEA

JUTLAND

Copenhagen ✪

Glasgow

Firth of Forth

Edinburgh

DENMARK

BALTIC SEA

Firth of Clyde

NORTHERN IRELAND

Belfast

Newcastle

HELGOLAND

Kiel

Swinemünde

UNITED KINGDOM

Kiel Canal

Hamburg

IRISH SEA

Hull

Wilhelmshaven

Berlin ✪

IRELAND

Liverpool

Bremen

North Channel

Saint George's Channel

ENGLAND

Birmingham

NETHERLANDS

Rotterdam

GERMANY

Bristol

London ✪

Strait of Dover

Cologne

Antwerp

Land's End

BELGIUM

English Channel

FRANCE

the Firth of Forth and the battleship *Nelson* at the entrance to Loch Ewe.

On their return to Wilhelmshaven, Prien and his crew received a hero's greeting from cheering crowds, brass bands, and two beaming admirals—Raeder and Dönitz—who presented them all with Iron Crosses. They were flown to Berlin for more parades, a news conference, and a ceremony in which Hitler presented Prien with the Knight's Cross.

More important for Dönitz, his delighted Führer eased the restrictions on U-boat warfare. Now any enemy merchant vessel could be attacked without warning, and passenger ships in convoy could be assaulted after an announcement of intentions. Privately, Dönitz had already told his commanders to sink any ship sailing without lights in waters where British vessels "are to be expected."

Dönitz's concern for the safety of his crews precipitated another harsh edict. On many occasions, his submariners had taken extreme measures in order to rescue the crews and passengers of ships that they had attacked. In October, off the coast of Ireland, the men of the U-35 removed the crew of the SS *Diamantis* before dispatching it to the deep, then took the time to tow the lifeboats to shore. Such efforts jeopardized his U-boats, Dönitz concluded, and he issued standing orders to his commanders to "rescue no one and take no one with you. Care only for your own boat and strive to achieve the next success as soon as possible! We must be hard in this war." Even so, some of his U-boat commanders continued to aid the crews of vessels they torpedoed.

The consequences of the U-boat war for Germany's enemies would have been disastrous had Dönitz's submarines been functioning properly. But it became increasingly apparent to him that something was disastrously wrong. Throughout September and October, reports on the scattered U-boat engagements frequently cited problems with torpedoes. At first, the troubles were attributed to green crews, but the longer the men were at sea, the less likely inexperience could be blamed. The failure of the redoubtable Günther Prien's first salvo in Scapa Flow raised further doubts about the torpedoes. Similar incidents followed.

On October 17, in one of the U-boat fleet's first coordinated attacks, three submarines fired repeatedly on a convoy but scored only a few hits. On October 30, the captain of the U-56 observed a procession of thirteen British warships—three battleships and ten destroyers. Summoning courage that bordered on foolhardiness, he stalked the powerful enemy task force, positioned the battleship *Nelson* in his sights, and launched three torpedoes. Just before he turned and ran for his life, he heard each torpedo hit the battleship—in a succession of dull thuds. There were no explosions.

Germany's celebration of the sinking of the British battleship *Royal Oak* at Scapa Flow begins as dockyard personnel welcome the U-47 back to Wilhelmshaven *(above, left)* on October 17. The Führer's private plane whisked all the crew members to Berlin, where they were paraded through the city *(above, right)*, and Hitler awarded their skipper, Günther Prien, the Knight's Cross of the Iron Cross *(right)*.

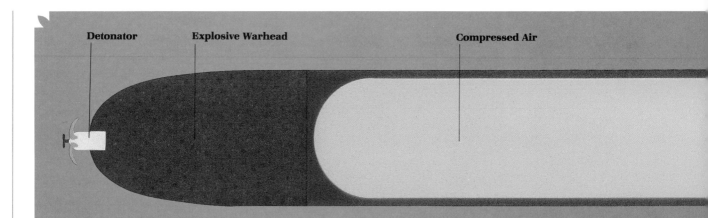

Detonator   Explosive Warhead   Compressed Air

Anatomy of a Torpedo

The torpedo Germany counted on to shred the sea lanes that sustained the British empire was an intricate machine, powered by its own engine and kept on course by a self-contained guidance system. The standard model used early in the war was the G7a *(above)*. Key to its operation was a tank of compressed air that took up nearly half the space inside the twenty-three-foot-long steel casing.

When the torpedo was launched, its passage through the boat's torpedo tube tripped an activating switch, and the air, initially compressed to almost 3,000 pounds per square inch of pressure, rushed backward through a slender pipe. Moderated by a pressure regulator, the air entered a combustion chamber and, flowing through additional tubes, also activated the torpedo's mechanical systems.

Inside the combustion chamber, a percussion igniter similar to a sparkplug fired a mixture of the pressurized air and fuel from a nearby tank. Turned to steam by a

The officer was made so distraught by the misfires that Dönitz had to reassign him to training duty.

By this time, the evidence was unmistakable. As Dönitz angrily wrote in his diary on October 31, *"At least* 30 percent of our torpedoes are duds. They do not detonate, or they detonate in the wrong place. Commanders must be losing confidence in their torpedoes." Even worse, he was losing boats at a rapid rate—seven by the end of October, all of them apparently caught on the surface. Such losses, he wrote, "must lead to the paralysis of U-boat warfare if no means can be devised of keeping them down."

Repairs to damaged submarines were taking longer than Dönitz had expected, and he was able to deploy only about a half-dozen U-boats in the Atlantic during the winter months of 1939-1940. Frustrated, he abandoned for the time being all efforts to inaugurate wolf-pack tactics against convoys. The British Admiralty took comfort from the statistics: "Out of 146 ships sunk during the first six months by U-boats, only 7 were in convoys escorted by antisubmarine vessels."

Through the winter, Dönitz struggled with his fleet's mechanical problems. Engine mountings on the type-VII boats were too light and failed prematurely, requiring longer refitting periods. The faulty design of the seawater valve on the engine exhausts was taking a toll; Dönitz surmised that dangerously leaking valves had forced some of the boats sunk by the enemy to surface while under attack.

The most critical flaws, however, were those afflicting the torpedoes. The torpedoes of World War I, powered by gasoline engines that were sustained by compressed air, had been simple and utterly reliable. But the exhaust of these engines had left a foamy wake that gave enemy ships a good chance

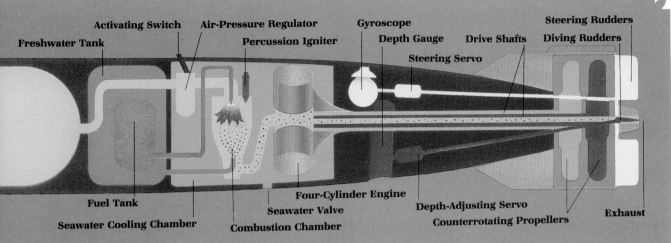

Freshwater Tank

Activating Switch

Air-Pressure Regulator

Percussion Igniter

Gyroscope

Depth Gauge

Steering Servo

Drive Shafts

Steering Rudders

Diving Rudders

Fuel Tank

Seawater Cooling Chamber

Combustion Chamber

Seawater Valve

Four-Cylinder Engine

Depth-Adjusting Servo

Counterrotating Propellers

Exhaust

fine spray of fresh water, the super-heated gases powered the torpedo's compact four-cylinder engine, which in turn spun a pair of hollow drive shafts, one inside the other. The shafts turned two propellers, which moved in opposite directions so as not to create torque that would warp the torpedo's course.

Keeping it on course was the job of the gyroscope, spun by com-pressed air at speeds that varied with the three preset speeds of the torpedo—thirty, forty, or forty-four knots. Able to sense any deviation from the torpedo's intended path, the gyro activated a tiny motor, or servo, that changed the setting of the steering rudders. A depth gauge and its servo kept the torpedo run-ning at the desired depth by ad-justing the diving rudders.

The warheads on early G7a tor-pedoes had relatively simple con-tact detonators, but even these boasted an ingenious mechanism: a small propeller that had to spin through ninety feet of water before the detonator was armed and ready to ignite the main charge of high explosive. This device guaranteed that the warhead did not explode prematurely, destroying the U-boat.

to avoid the torpedo and then track down the boat that had fired it. The use of new, exhaust-free electric motors solved that problem, but redesign of the weapon had introduced new flaws.

Early torpedoes had been detonated exclusively by contact; when they hit a ship, a simple firing pin set off an explosive charge. In the newer models, the mechanism had been replaced by a more complex device that used a series of levers and linkages to transfer the blow. This new detonator failed often, for unknown reasons, and never worked if the torpedo struck its target at an oblique angle.

Now the mechanically fired torpedoes were being rendered obsolete, supposedly, by a recently invented magnetic trigger. This type of detonator contained a sensor that ignited the torpedo in response to the magnetic field of a ship overhead. Theoretically, the torpedo would explode directly under the ship, where the shock would break the keel, inflicting far more damage than a burst against the side of the hull. In practice, however, the magnetic torpedoes were proving tricky: They were firing early, firing late, or firing not at all. It was discovered that physical shocks could set them off, making them a menace to the submarine firing them. Variations in the earth's magnetism or the presence of ores under the seafloor could also seriously affect their adjustment. Moreover, for some reason, both the mechanical and the magnetic torpedoes ran too deep—much deeper than their designated settings.

Dönitz had hardly begun to define all these problems, let alone solve them, when his fleet was given a crucial new assignment. Late in 1939, Hitler decided to postpone his planned offensive in western Europe in order to invade Norway and Denmark. The change of plans was largely

Mastering the Marksman's Art

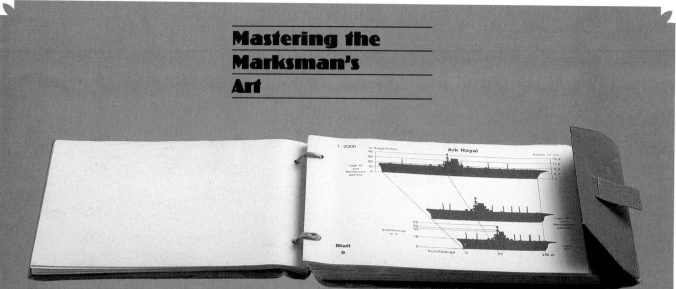

The carrier *Ark Royal* appears at three angles in a U-boat's identification book.

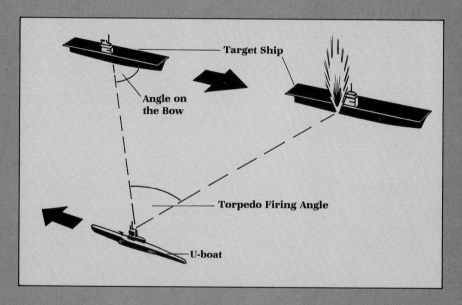

Contrary to popular notion, hitting a moving target with a torpedo from a platform as unstable as a submarine was not easy. It required nerve, patience, synchronized teamwork, and a gift for marksmanship that some skippers seemed born with and others never attained.

The challenge began when the four-man bridge watch sighted a ship coming over the horizon. Was it friend or foe, warship or cargo vessel? What was its draught? (This fact would determine how deep a torpedo should run.) U-boat officers learned to recognize ship silhouettes and always carried a handbook *(top)* that showed hostile

ships broadside and from bow angles of forty-five and sixty degrees.

More demanding was figuring the speed and direction of a distant vessel and calculating how to hit it at a range and bearing that changed frequently. The maneuvering for position might take days. A straight shot was simplest—aiming the bow where the target should be when the torpedo arrived and firing dead ahead—but conditions seldom permitted this. Instead, submarines often fired while moving parallel to or even away from the target, dispatching the torpedo at an angle, as shown in the diagram above.

Angle shots were possible to cal-

culate because U-boats carried a torpedo data computer. This mechanical calculator absorbed such information as the U-boat's position and the captain's estimate of the target's speed, range, and course. Doing the needed math— and updating it as the variables changed—the calculator passed its solution electrically to the torpedo rooms, where crewmen cranked the firing angle into the torpedo's gyroscope. Once launched, the torpedo ran straight for a few yards, then turned to follow the gyro's preset angle to where—if captain, calculator, and crew had done their jobs—it would intercept its victim.

influenced by the arguments of Admiral Raeder. The two Scandinavian countries were critically important to the German navy because they commanded the strategic Skagerrak—the bottleneck entrance to the Baltic Sea. Norway's rugged coastline, within easy reach of the North Atlantic, also offered ideal harbors for warships and submarines. In addition, more than half the iron ore arriving at the steel mills of the Reich came from Sweden, and in the winter months, it had to be shipped by way of the northern Norwegian port of Narvik.

Hitler would have preferred to let Norway remain neutral, but intelligence reports warning of an imminent British invasion of the country finally persuaded him to attack. On February 5, Dönitz was ordered to make plans for protecting the German invasion force from the British fleet. The Führer vacillated until April 1, then ordered the assault for April 9. The operation was audacious and meticulously planned. In the predawn darkness, German ships laden with troops sailed into all five of Norway's major seaports, and the stunned country quickly found its ports, airfields, and communications networks in the hands of the invaders. The Norwegians gamely began to fight back; the Danes, however, offered little resistance and were overrun within hours.

By sheer coincidence, the German invasion fleet ran into a British naval expedition that had mined the offshore channel known as the Leads, through which Swedish iron ore was transported south to Germany. In most of the nautical skirmishes that ensued, German vessels took a hammering. Five British destroyers sailed into Narvik harbor on April 10 and sank two German destroyers, damaged three more, and then sank all the cargo ships in sight, save one. Five more German destroyers came on the scene and drove the attackers off, but three days later, a British battleship arrived at Narvik with a flotilla of destroyers and sank almost everything German in the harbor. Only a supply ship remained afloat.

Still, the Germans remained firmly in control of Narvik and other key seaports. In an effort to dislodge them, the British mounted an expedition force and sent troops ashore at key coastal points. Many of the men in the first landings were ill-trained Territorials. They carried only two days' supplies and lacked essential maps and equipment. None of the British had skis, and without them, movement across the snowbound Norwegian countryside was almost impossible. The troops failed to make much headway against the entrenched Germans. At sea, however, the story was different, as Raeder's navy continued to sustain heavy losses.

Dönitz's U-boats were supposed to prevent such casualties, but they were having troubles of their own. Dönitz had gathered every submarine afloat, a total of thirty-one. He placed two to five boats off each target port, but he expected little from their performance in the narrow fjords and tricky waters. His main effort was to be made by larger groups of boats massed off Norway's southwest coast and in the waters close to the Shetland and Orkney islands, where British warships and troop transports coming to Norway's relief would have to pass.

The British destroyers that ravaged Narvik sailed right past the guarding U-boats in a driving snowstorm. The luck of the submarines grew worse when the British recovered a map of the U-boat dispositions from a German vessel and used it to avoid their submerged enemy. The most frustrating experiences, however, were reserved for those U-boat captains who managed to make contact with the British.

On April 15, Günther Prien, in the U-47, came upon a British landing force going ashore from six huge transports in a tiny fjord. The transports and their destroyer escort were sitting ducks, and Prien carefully fired all four of his forward torpedoes at them. Not one torpedo exploded. The British still did not know the U-boat was there. Prien reloaded his tubes. He and his officers checked every setting and adjustment with infinite care, and after midnight he tried again. Three more torpedoes whirred into the dark water, never again to be heard from. A fourth, however, did explode—after veering crazily off course and ramming into a cliff. The alarmed destroyers responded with volley after volley of depth charges, almost sinking the U-47 before Prien could get away.

Not only was the experience typical, it was universal. German U-boats launched thirty-eight attacks during the Norwegian operation and sank one ship, a transport. Nearly half of the torpedoes with magnetic detonators exploded prematurely; almost none of those with mechanical detonators exploded at all. The only thing in the U-boat fleet that blew up with any predictability was Karl Dönitz. The performance of the torpedoes was "intolerable," he raged, "an absurdity. In effect, the boats are unarmed. I do not believe that ever in the history of war have men been sent against the enemy with such useless weapons."

Dönitz recalled his U-boats and demanded an investigation. Raeder complied, and a month later, when the fighting in Norway had sputtered out, the British had withdrawn, and the Germans were firmly in control, the findings of a special U-boat commission made Dönitz even angrier. "The facts," he wrote at the time, "are worse than could have been expected." The new magnetic detonators, the commission found, had been rushed into production after a testing program that involved the firing of only two torpedoes, with imperfect results. The commission also declared that the redesigned mechanical detonators had become so complicated that malfunctioning was to be expected. Dönitz banned the magnetic

Back from patrol, a young U-boat commander *(left)* reports personally to Dönitz and his adjutant *(in white uniform)*. Dönitz had been promoted to rear admiral in recognition of his U-boats' early successes.

detonators and demanded that a simpler, more reliable mechanical firing pin be supplied immediately. At that, the problems with the torpedoes had not yet been fully explored. It would take another two years to discover an elemental design flaw in the device that regulated the depth at which the torpedoes ran. Depth depended on a balance chamber that was supposed to contain air at standard atmospheric pressure but was so leaky that it admitted pressurized air from the submerged submarine, causing the torpedoes to run several feet deeper than their setting.

Even if Dönitz had been able to correct the torpedoes in April of 1940, his fleet would still have been ineffective. The first eight months of war had battered his boats and exhausted his crews. The sailors needed recuperation and their craft extensive repairs. It would be June before he would have a workable complement of boats on station in the Atlantic again. Meanwhile, the war reeled on. ✠

Inside a Captured Predator

To enter a U-boat was to descend into an underworld of confounding complexity. One ensign described his first halting steps after reporting aboard: "I banged my head against pipes and ducts, against handwheels and instruments, against the low, round hatches in bulkheads that separated the compartments. It was like crawling through the neck of a bottle." As others confirmed, a U-boat was designed not for human comfort but to house the machinery needed to drive the vessel and deliver its deadly payload. The typical submarine was barely twenty feet wide, and its interior was further constricted by the gap between the outer and inner hulls—a space containing fuel tanks and cells that could be flooded with water to submerge the vessel or filled with air to buoy it.

Germany shrouded its U-boat program in secrecy, but on rare occasions disabled boats were seized intact. In June 1944, a U.S. Navy task group commanded by Captain Daniel V. Gallery crippled and captured the U-505—a 252-foot-long, type-IXC vessel able to carry twenty-two torpedoes. The Americans boarded the U-505 and took it in tow (right). The boat yielded valuable data to the Allies and later became a permanent exhibit at Chicago's Museum of Science and Industry. The U-505 contained a series of compartments (labeled below) connected by hatches that could be sealed in an emergency. Torpedo rooms at the bow and stern doubled as the crew's barracks. The space in between housed the officers; the galley; the sonar, radio, and control rooms; diesel engines for running on the surface; and electric motors for cruising in the depths.

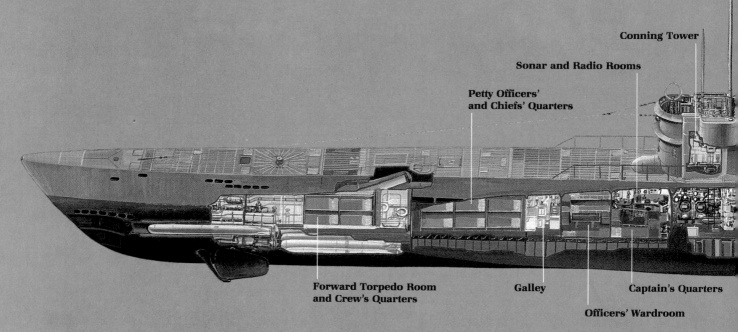

Conning Tower

Sonar and Radio Rooms

Petty Officers'
and Chiefs' Quarters

Forward Torpedo Room
and Crew's Quarters

Galley

Captain's Quarters

Officers' Wardroom

Control Roo

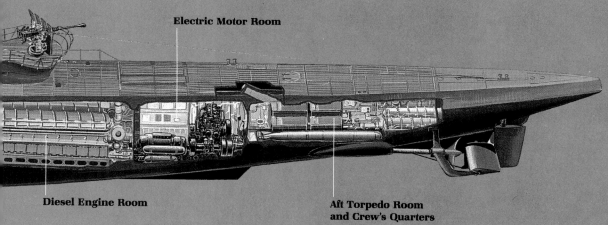

Electric Motor Room

Diesel Engine Room

**Aft Torpedo Room
and Crew's Quarters**

At left, a view of the U-505's forward torpedo room, facing the bow, shows one of the twenty-one-foot-long projectiles positioned for loading into a tube beyond the folding bunks. Each bunk was shared by two members of the crew, who worked and slept in alternate shifts. When the boat was fully armed, four torpedoes lay ready for firing in the bow tubes, and five more were held here in reserve. Eight were stored in tubes outside the pressure hull and five in the aft torpedo room.

Above, the bow tubes of the U-505 are displayed in four stages of readiness: clockwise from lower left, tube plugged, tube open for loading, torpedo partially inserted, and torpedo fully inserted and propeller visible. On firing, a charge of compressed air ejected the torpedo from the tube. Then the projectile's electric motor took over, powering the warhead to its target at a speed of thirty knots while leaving no trail of exhaust for the enemy to spot.

Galley and Officers' Wardroom

In the galley below, equipped with an electric stove and a sink that provided a limited supply of fresh water distilled from salt water, the cook prepared meals for the U-505's complement of up to sixty officers and crew. Only a few perishables could be kept fresh in the small refrigerators.

Individual bunks and handsome storage compartments, including a glass-paned cupboard, distinguished the officers' wardroom from the crew's quarters. But the officers enjoyed no more privacy than the enlisted men; traffic passed freely through their centrally located compartment.

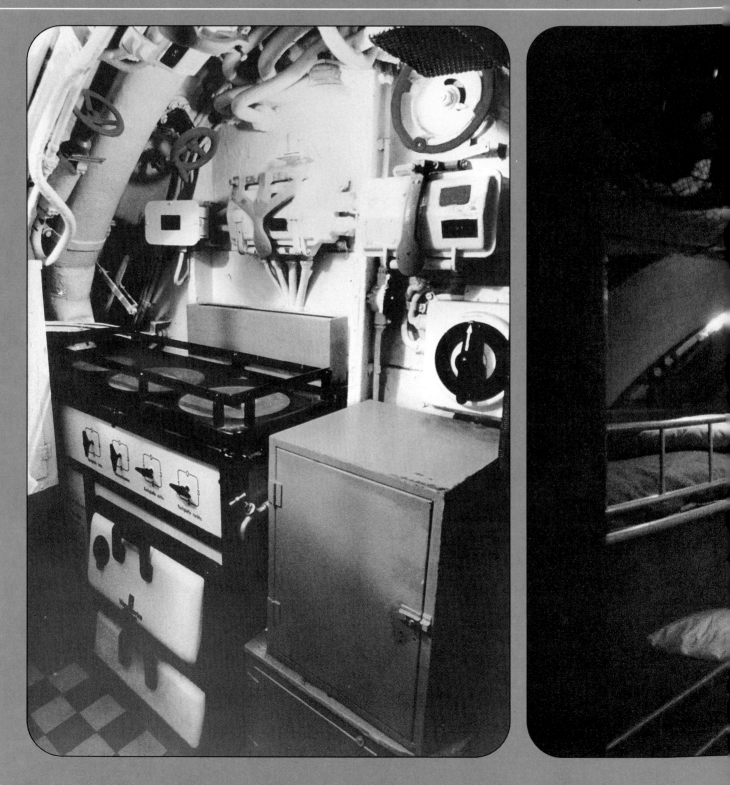

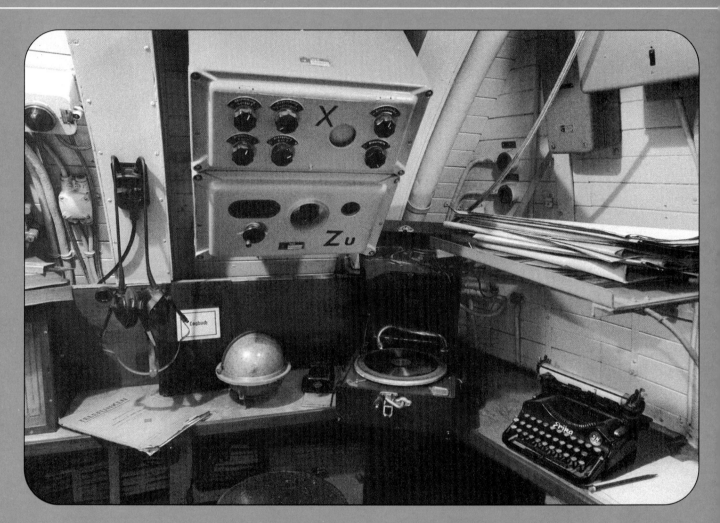

In the small space above, located across the passageway from the captain's quarters, an operator wearing the headphones hanging at left sent and received coded signals over the radio equipment at top. Other items included a globe, a typewriter, and a phonograph connected to the boat's loudspeaker system.

The captain's quarters (*right*) featured ample storage space, a speaking tube, and a washstand whose lid could be lowered to form a writing table. The captain could sequester himself here by drawing a curtain, but he spent much of the day in full view of his men, who relied on him to present a calm, decisive front.

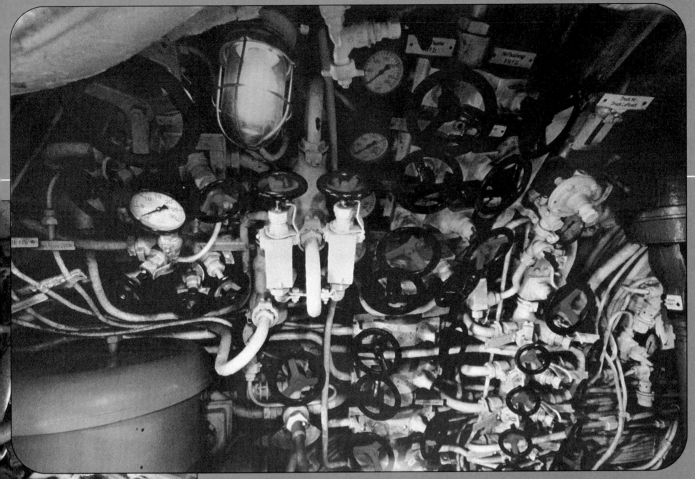

The control room—a maze of valves, gauges, handwheels, and pipes—was the U-boat's nerve center, where technicians steered and stabilized the vessel and monitored its vital signs. To escape detection, crewmen turned the two large wheels *(left)* to adjust the hydroplanes at the bow and stern that caused the boat to rise or descend. Valves on the bulkheads and the overhead *(above)* regulated the movement of air under normal or high pressure for a host of essential functions. The ladder at the center of the room led to the conning tower, where the captain operated the navigation and attack periscopes. His orders were relayed from the control room to other compartments through speaking tubes attached to the periscope shaft *(below)*.

When running on the surface, the U-505 was powered by two nine-cylinder, 2,170-horsepower diesel engines *(right)* that turned a pair of propellers at the stern, generating a top speed of nineteen knots. The diesels also turned the dynamotors in the adjoining chamber *(following pages)*, recharging the batteries for the electric power plant. Each diesel had its own set of controls and monitors *(left)*, including separate temperature gauges for the nine cylinders, which were cooled by seawater. The dial of the engine-order telegraph *(near left)* indicated the desired speed and direction of the U-boat, as communicated electronically from the control room or conning tower—ranging from full speed ahead to stop, reverse, or the alarm signal, Dive! This enabled the engineers to respond immediately, without awaiting hand signals or straining to pick up spoken commands over the din of the diesels.

Electric Motor Room

Among the most vital organs in the anatomy of the U-boat was the air compressor (*below, left*), powered by one of the electric motors in the picture at right. Compressed air was required to prime the diesel engine, discharge the torpedoes from their tubes, and blow water from the ballast tanks between the inner and outer hulls for swift ascents.

The U-boat's electric plant (*below, right*) consisted of two dynamotors—one on each side of the passageway—and a control panel, visible to the left of the watertight door. When the sub was on the surface, with diesels churning, the dynamotors functioned as generators to charge the boat's batteries; when the vessel submerged, the batteries returned the energy to drive the dynamotors, providing a maximum speed of 7.5 knots.

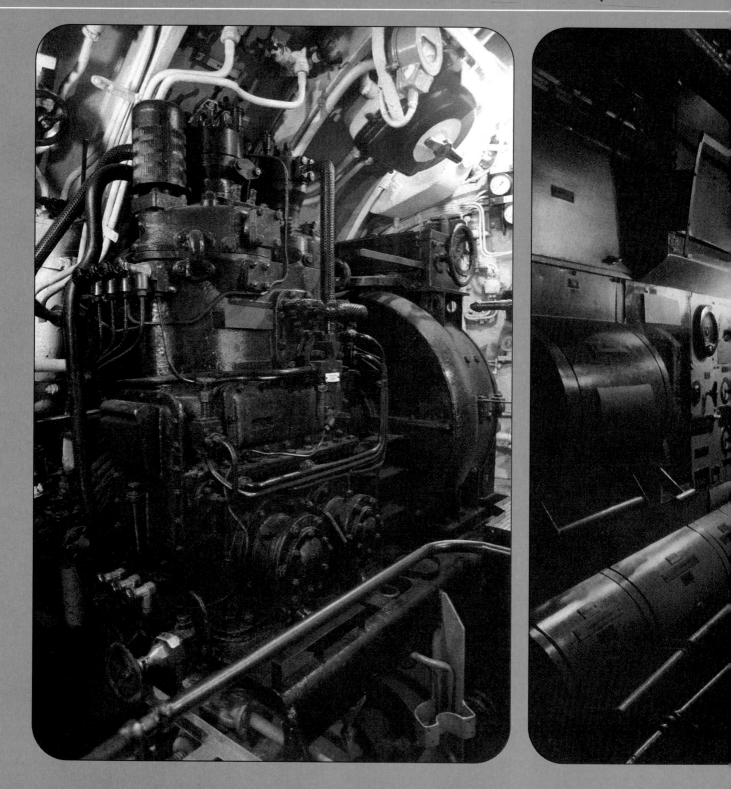

Aft Torpedo Room and Crew's Quarters

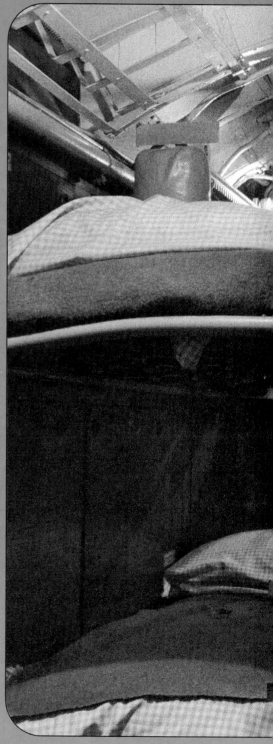

The U-505 was equipped with two toilets, one in the forward torpedo room and the other in the aft torpedo room. Crew members often had to wait their turn, since the forward head was usually packed with provisions or reserved for sick crew members. At depths below eighty feet, neither head could be flushed, and a bucket in the diesel engine room served instead.

The aft torpedo room contained eight bunks for sixteen crewmen, two torpedo tubes (*background*), and an auxiliary steering wheel that was operated manually in case the main steering mechanism, located in the control room, failed. Living and working in such close quarters was complicated by the fact that the U-boat operated most of the time on the surface, pitching and yawing. Unless a man strapped himself to his bunk in rough seas, one veteran recalled, he might find himself sharing a berth with his shipmate across the way.

A Time for Aces

The conquest of Norway earned Germany a key operational base in the warming struggle with Great Britain, opened the Atlantic Ocean to the German navy, and guaranteed an uninterrupted flow of iron ore from neutral Sweden to Hitler's war industries. For the undersea arm, however, the campaign had been a frustrating setback. Not only had Rear Admiral Dönitz been forced to shelve what he considered the U-boats' primary mission—putting a fatal stranglehold on Britain's oceanic lifeline—but four of his thirty-one submarines had been lost while sinking a single enemy ship. Angry and dejected, the surviving crews blamed faulty torpedoes for their disastrous performance. Time and time again, U-boat commanders had maneuvered their craft into attack position in the confined coastal waters only to watch their magnetic torpedoes run too deep, explode at the wrong time, or fail to explode at all. Günther Prien, the hero of Scapa Flow, complained bitterly that he could not fight armed "with a dummy rifle." Eberhard Godt, Dönitz's chief of operations, argued mutinously that the U-boat command would be justified in refusing to put to sea until improvements were made. The self-confidence so important to men going to war in submarines began to shrivel; Dönitz wrote that his captains and crews had slipped into a "slough of despond."

During the following weeks, while most of his U-boats were in dockyards being serviced, Dönitz sought to lift his men out of their doldrums. He visited operational flotillas and training bases, mingling with crew members and reassuring them that their mission was still within reach. But to prove his claim, Dönitz needed a success. The first opportunity came on May 15, 1940, when he ordered Lieut. Commander Victor Oehrn to take the U-37 into the North Atlantic from its base at Wilhelmshaven. Armed with a combination of the unreliable magnetic torpedoes and improved contact-percussion types, the U-37 was the first German submarine in three months to venture into the Atlantic. Oehrn's instructions were to prowl the Western Approaches, the waters northwest of Cape Finisterre at the western end of the English Channel—a natural hunting ground. In addition to sinking as much enemy tonnage as possible, Oehrn was to gather intelligence

A U-boat's lookout watches a torpedoed merchant ship go down as the submarine closes in on the vessel's companion. In the months after the conquest of France, U-boats preyed ceaselessly on cargo ships that crossed the Atlantic unescorted or with minimal protection.

about British antisubmarine defenses. Had the British changed shipping routes? Where did the supply ships pick up their escorts and how strong were they? How far out did enemy air patrols extend?

Although Oehrn had never commanded a U-boat on war patrol, he was a solid choice for the assignment. During the previous eighteen months, he had served as operations officer at Dönitz's headquarters and had impressed the U-boat commander in chief with his "exceptionally clear and determined mind"; it was Oehrn who had convinced Dönitz of the feasibility of sending Prien's U-47 into Scapa Flow. Moreover, the desk-bound officer was eager to test his mettle in combat.

Dönitz's confidence in Oehrn paid off handsomely. At the start of the patrol, the magnetic torpedoes failed again (causing Dönitz to ban their further use). Nevertheless, in twenty-six days at sea, the U-37 sank eleven ships totaling more than 43,000 tons. The mission demonstrated that British shipping was still highly vulnerable. "The spell of bad luck was broken," Dönitz later wrote. "The fighting powers of the U-boat had once again been proved. Now the other U-boats put to sea convinced that they, too, could do what the U-37 had done. Psychologically, the effects of the Norwegian failures had been overcome."

Oehrn's maiden voyage launched a five-month-long stretch of unprecedented success. In June 1940, although no more than six submarines were at sea and hunting at any one time, Dönitz's so-called gray wolves destroyed thirty ships totaling 284,113 tons, the highest monthly figure to date. No U-boats were lost. Prien and the U-47, flaunting a snorting-bull insignia on its conning tower, alone claimed more than 66,000 tons. It was the beginning of what submariners would warmly remember as the *Glückliche Zeit*, or Happy Time.

Soon other aces emerged. In July, the U-99's commander, Otto Kretschmer, a taciturn taskmaster nicknamed Otto the Silent by his men, sank seven ships on a single patrol. In August, the U-100's Joachim Schepke, a handsome bon vivant, sent five ships to the bottom in three hours of fighting. That same month, Dönitz received a shot in the arm when the High Command of the Wehrmacht announced a total blockade of the British Isles and dropped the last restrictions on U-boat warfare. Henceforth, U-boats could sink without warning any ship that happened into range.

The tactical balance between hunter and hunted had tilted sharply in favor of the hunter. The occupation of Norway and much of France gave Germany command of the European seaboard from the northern reaches of the Norwegian Sea to the Bay of Biscay. Submarine bases would soon be established in Norway at Bergen, Trondheim, Kristiansund, and Narvik,

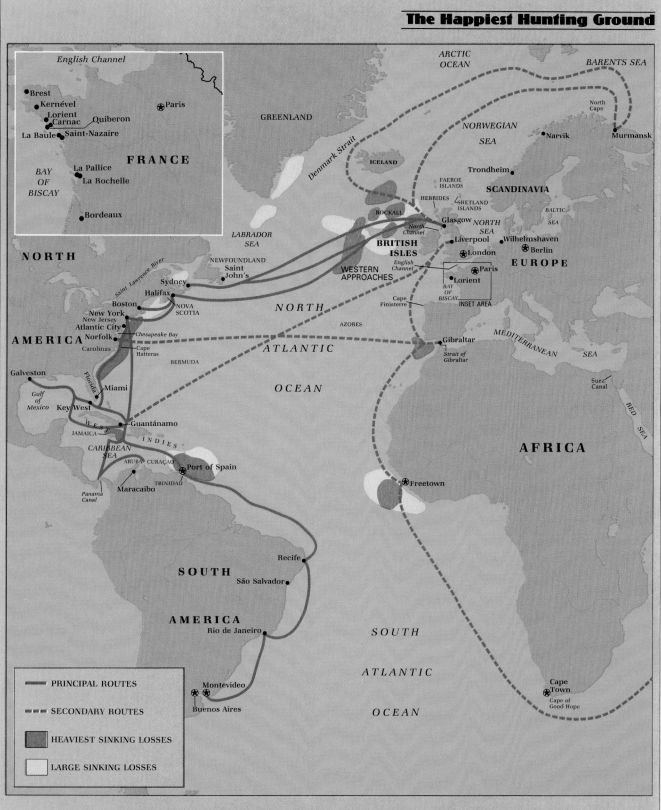

PRINCIPAL ROUTES

SECONDARY ROUTES

HEAVIEST SINKING LOSSES

LARGE SINKING LOSSES

The conquest of France in June 1940 transformed the U-boat war. By taking over the ports at Brest, Lorient, La Pallice, Saint-Nazaire, La Rochelle, and Bordeaux on the Bay of Biscay (*inset*), the U-boats were able to expand their offensive against Allied shipping from the Western Approaches, near Ireland and Scotland, where convoys bound for Britain converged, to the open Atlantic. Eventually, German submarines ranged into the Mediterranean Sea, the waters off West Africa and the eastern United States, and the Caribbean Sea. The wolf packs concentrated their attacks on the main shipping routes shown here. Areas where the U-boats sank the most merchant ships are indicated in yellow, with the heaviest losses in orange.

and in France at Brest, Lorient, Bordeaux, La Pallice, La Rochelle, and Saint-Nazaire. No longer could the British fleet bottle up the U-boats by blocking the North Sea exits, as the Royal Navy had done successfully in World War I. In the south, the route to Gibraltar, used by Allied shipping from the South Atlantic and the Indian Ocean, was now outflanked by the German-held ports on the Bay of Biscay.

More important, operating from the French ports reduced the time U-boats had to spend in transit. Before Germany's stunning blitzkrieg victory, its submarines had to sail 450 miles through the North Sea and around the north coast of Scotland to the Atlantic. Now they could reach the ocean faster and hunt the enemy as much as a week longer before returning to the convenient dockyards of France. Making the U-boats' job still easier, the British, responding to the threat of Luftwaffe attacks, re-routed convoys through the North Channel between Ireland and Scotland. The resulting bottleneck provided abundant, slow-moving prey.

British antisubmarine defenses were stretched thin. Destroyers and other escort ships of the Royal Navy that had participated in the Norwegian campaign were laid up for refitting. Many small craft capable of antisub-marine duty had been lost in the evacuation of Dunkirk. British ships had to be deployed in the English Channel to defend against an anticipated German invasion. As a result, from May to October 1940, the British were able to escort outbound convoys only as far as 12°W longitude, roughly 100 miles beyond Ireland, and pick up inbound convoys at the same point. Canadian destroyers escorted convoys from North America only 400 miles eastward into the Atlantic; from there, the ships had to sail hundreds of miles with no more than a lone auxiliary cruiser as protection until a British escort picked them up at the 12°W rendezvous. That left an immense gap in the mid-Atlantic where U-boats could attack with impunity. The British occupied Iceland in May 1940, and in September the United States gave Britain fifty overage destroyers in exchange for bases in Newfoundland, Bermuda, and the West Indies. But the transaction came too late to help Allied merchant shipping during the summer of 1940.

Dönitz moved quickly to exploit his new advantages. Even as German panzers sliced through northern France in May, he had a train standing by in Germany, loaded with torpedoes and all the necessary maintenance personnel and matériel to set up shop on the Bay of Biscay. On June 23, the day after France signed an armistice, the U-boat chief traveled to the Biscay bases to check them out firsthand. On July 7, the U-30, skippered by Lieut. Commander Fritz-Julius Lemp (who had sunk the liner *Athenia* on the first day of war), became the first to return from the Atlantic directly to a French base, Lorient. By August 2, the dockyard there had geared up

Focusing on an electric meter, students at a submarine school learn a rudimentary lesson in maintaining their boat's electric motors. Cables connect the one-cell battery *(center)* to the meter. When the cable switch is closed, current flows from battery to meter, and the pointer registers its strength. As the battery wears down, the current decreases and the pointer edges toward zero. By reading a U-boat's meters, members of the crew could de-termine when the crucial batteries had to be recharged.

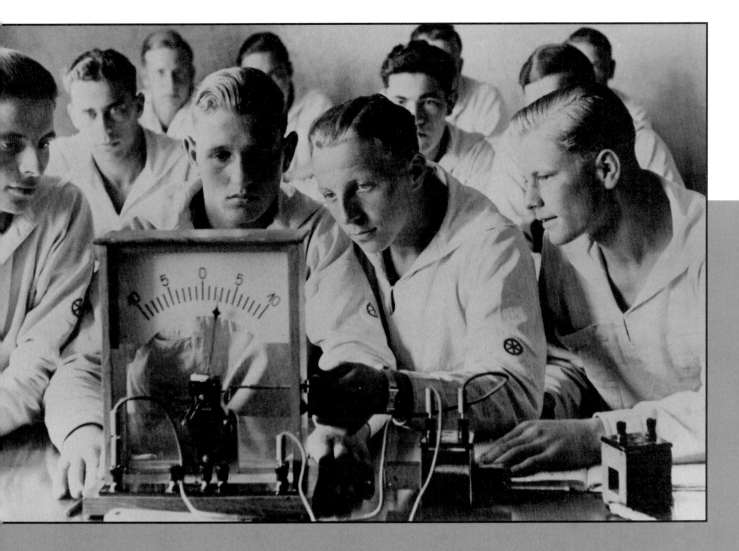

Training a Seagoing Elite

After they had completed basic naval training, U-boat recruits attended submarine schools in order to prepare for an arduous life at sea. Teamwork, skill, and the ability to work in a hostile environment were crucial to a crew's success and survival, and instructors looked for and developed these qualities in their students. Those who were found wanting—nearly 90 percent—were dismissed from the tough course.

In the first phase of their training, all recruits devoted twelve-hour days to physical conditioning and classroom instruction on the inner workings of a U-boat. They ab-sorbed sighting techniques, navigation, the theory of torpedo firing and artillery, how to operate radios, diesel engines, electric motors, and air compressors, and—perhaps most important—how to open and close hatches in an emergency.

In the second phase of training, the recruits specialized. An officer candidate, for example, went to sea as a watch officer aboard an operational U-boat, then returned to shore for command training before taking charge of his own U-boat. Crewmen, meanwhile, trained in such ratings as torpedo mechanic, engineer, and radio operator.

A new commander and his designated crew visited the shipyard where their boat was being built to study it while still under construction. Once finished, the boat became the vehicle for their hands-on training. For two months, captain and crew practiced diving and wolf-pack maneuvers. They learned to cope with such emergencies as jammed rudders, losses of compressed air, pump breakdowns, and water leaks. Combat situations were also simulated, but in the relatively calm waters of the Baltic Sea, rather than in the rough Atlantic.

The demanding program produced a cadre of superb undersea warriors. By 1943, however, submarine losses were mounting dramatically, and less-qualified men joined the U-boat arm. On-board training time was slashed to get boats and crews into combat faster. The result was needless operational errors and still-higher casualty rates. Many an untried skipper relied on headquarters to make his critical decisions for him, a practice that continued, often with costly consequences, until the war's end.

Judging range and the angle on the bow of an enemy ship—moving either toward or away from a U-boat—was a critical skill. In the classroom exercise shown here, a technician (right), following instructions received through a headset, rotates a model ship while student officers (above) use high-powered binoculars to estimate the angle and—based on how much of the ship can be seen above the horizon—how far away it is.

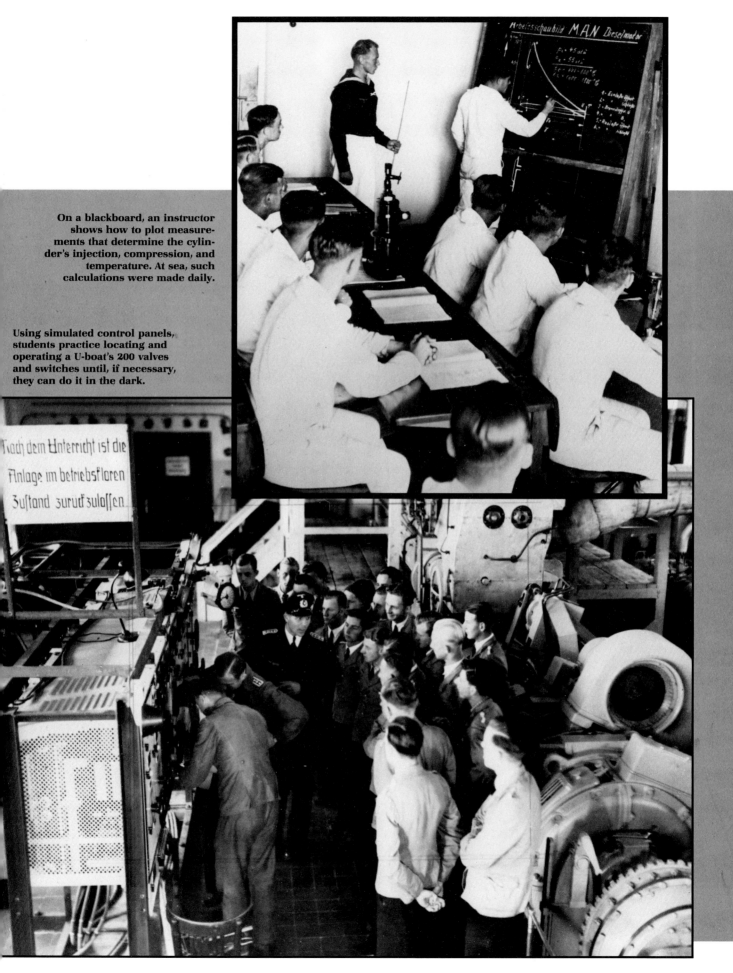

On a blackboard, an instructor shows how to plot measurements that determine the cylinder's injection, compression, and temperature. At sea, such calculations were made daily.

Using simulated control panels, students practice locating and operating a U-boat's 200 valves and switches until, if necessary, they can do it in the dark.

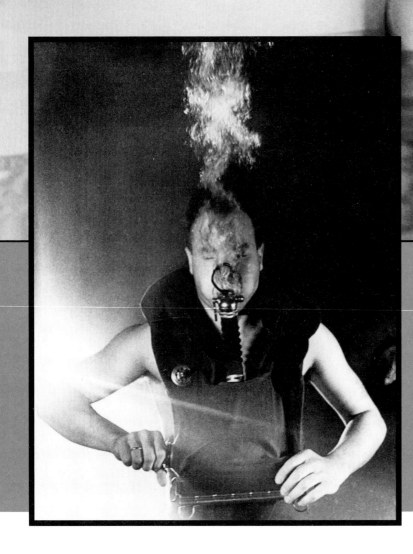

Inside a diving tank, a student practices breathing underwater with an artificial lung. To obtain oxygen stored in a cylinder inside his vest, he quickly opens and closes a side valve, inhales, and then exhales through a small vent in his face mask. A safety valve below his right shoulder serves as a backup for disposing of the carbon dioxide. Artificial lungs were used for making underwater repairs and emergency escapes from depths up to 400 feet.

to repair damaged boats, and henceforth all German U-boats operating in the Atlantic put in at ports in France instead of Germany.

Dönitz by now was running the submarine war from a block-long building on the Boulevard Suchet overlooking the Bois de Boulogne in Paris, where he had come to prepare for Operation Sea Lion, the projected invasion of England. He was determined that not a day should pass without at least one of his boats sinking an enemy ship. But before one could be sunk, it had to be found. If two days went by without sightings, he would radio his boats to try another stretch of the wide Atlantic.

Almost from the outbreak of war, the U-boat command was remarkably well informed about the makeup and movements of Allied convoys. A special radio-deciphering section, called B-Dienst, or B-Service, in the High Command of the Navy had broken the British naval codes. Given time, German cryptographers could pinpoint convoy routes, rendezvous locations, and escort strengths. Dönitz also received information through an incredible security lapse in the United States. American shipping-insurance companies continued to pool their underwriting risks with European companies. As a matter of course, the Americans wired detailed shipping information, including all pertinent data about the war matériel going to Britain, to their business partners. One recipient was an underwriter in Zurich who routinely passed it to an associate in Munich, who in turn relayed it to German naval intelligence. It was not until early 1943, more than a year after the United States had entered the war, that the U.S. Espionage Act required insurance companies to stop the practice.

As efficient as B-Dienst was, Dönitz conceded that deciphering convoy radio signals in time to organize wolf packs was largely a "matter of luck." In September of 1940, after several missed opportunities, he finally got lucky. His cryptographers intercepted signals describing a convoy-escort rendezvous early enough for him to detail four U-boats to the area. On September 10, despite heavy seas and gale-force winds, they sank five Allied ships, the first successful wolf-pack operation of the war. Eleven days later, another pack of five boats had even better hunting: Attacking a fifteen-ship convoy, the U-boats sank eleven ships and crippled a twelfth.

Then Dönitz hit the jackpot. On the night of October 16-17, Lieut. Commander Heinrich Bleichrodt in the U-48 was patrolling northwest of Rockall, about 200 miles west of the Hebrides, when he sighted a large convoy heading east. Designated SC7, the convoy consisted of thirty-two heavily laden merchant ships en route to Britain from Sydney, Nova Scotia. Bleichrodt radioed U-boat command in Paris, and Dönitz ordered five more boats to the area; they included Kretschmer's U-99 and Schepke's U-100. Bleichrodt sank two of the convoy. Then its escorts attacked him, and he lost

A brass band and an honor guard lend a festive air to the departure of the U-29 as it glides out of the new German submarine base at Lorient, in occupied France, during the fall of 1940.

contact. Dönitz made an educated guess. He directed the five converging boats to set up a north-south patrol line far to the east of the convoy's last known position. By daylight on October 18, the U-boats were in position, several miles from one another. That night, the convoy steamed into Dönitz's line, and, under a full moon and in calm seas, the wolves attacked.

Once a U-boat attack began, individual commanders were free to use any tactics they chose. Most stayed outside the escort screen, hunting along the flanks of the convoy. When they found a target, they would fire off a fan-shaped pattern of three or four torpedoes. Kretschmer, however, had perfected a tactic of his own: He liked to head straight for the center of the convoy. Slipping past the escorts, he would knife through the inside columns of merchant ships, picking them off one by one, firing a single torpedo at a time at relatively close range. Whatever the tactics employed, the strategy was generally the same: Attack at night, when the shapes of cargo ships bulked large and a U-boat's low silhouette was barely visible; remain on the surface, where the asdic of the convoy escorts could not locate the submarine and the U-boat could take advantage of its speed and maneuverability; and fire from as close as possible.

At 8:15 p.m., Lieut. Commander Engelbert Endrass's U-46 scored the first hit against a 2,000-ton Swedish merchantman in the convoy. Buoyed by a cargo of pulpwood, the victim remained afloat at a crazy angle for fifteen minutes, bow pointing to the sky, before going down. Over the next two hours, the wolf pack destroyed eight more ships. Those with cargoes of steel or pig iron sank immediately. Others, loaded with timber, went up in flames, the force of the explosions scattering planks high into the air, littering the sea. As torpedoes continued to strike their targets, blast after blast lit up the sky. Smoke from burning ships billowed hundreds of feet into the air. Flares from the escort vessels and merchantmen streaked across the horizon. Occasionally, ships' sirens pierced the air as vessels in the convoy, desperately evading torpedoes, narrowly avoided collisions. And against the backdrop of chaos and destruction, lifeboats and rafts bobbed on the surface, their tiny lights twinkling eerily.

"The destroyers are at their wit's end," Kretschmer wrote in his war diary during the attack on SC7, "shooting off star shells the whole time to comfort themselves and each other." The convoy escort, consisting of only three ships, was inexperienced and could do nothing else against the swift, nearly invisible U-boats running wild in their midst. Around three o'clock in the morning, after three of the five submarines had fired all of their torpedoes, the pack broke off its attack. In seven hours, seventeen ships, more than half of the convoy, had been sunk.

Dönitz and his crews were not content. Only sixteen hours after the last

SC7 ship had been sent to the bottom, a second wolf pack tore into another hapless convoy. This one, sighted by Prien's U-47 about 250 miles west of the scene of SC7's destruction, was the HX79. It consisted of forty-nine cargo ships and twelve escorts en route from Halifax, Nova Scotia. Dönitz deployed Prien, Endrass, Schepke, Bleichrodt, and Lieut. Commander Heinrich Liebe in the U-38. By dawn, when the U-boats slipped away, they had sunk twelve ships.

In little more than thirty hours, ten U-boats operating in two wolf packs had destroyed twenty-nine enemy ships without a single loss of their own. Back home, German newspapers jubilantly trumpeted the twin exploits. For Dönitz, who had never doubted the validity of attacking in groups, the night only reconfirmed the correctness of his judgment.

In November, Dönitz moved his headquarters from Paris to a country château in Kernével, twenty-five miles northwest of the port of Lorient. Inside the château, all U-boat operations were planned and directed from two situation rooms. The walls were covered with coded grid maps. Colored pins and flags marked the location of each boat at sea as well as each known enemy convoy and naval vessel. Charts and diagrams indicated a mass of variables that had to be factored into the decision-making process: the time differences between Lorient and the U-boats, the weather, the tides, ice and fog conditions.

There was also a third room, called the Museum. Here the walls were adorned with graphs comparing U-boat losses and enemy ships sunk. One could tell at a glance how the war at sea was going. The key graph for Dönitz was one that showed the "effective U-boat quotient"—the average tonnage sunk per day per submarine at sea. He compared it to the temperature chart at the foot of a patient's bed. Dönitz knew that the kill figures his commanders provided were often exaggerated. Nonetheless, the graph provided an accurate picture of the monthly rise and fall of the U-boat campaign. The estimates were reasonably close to the figures calculated later from statistics of actual sinkings released by the British: Tonnage sunk per U-boat per day at sea in June was 514; in July, 594; in August, 664; in September, 758; and in October, the month of the big convoy battles, 920.

Despite these victories, as the first year of fighting ended, Dönitz must have had mixed feelings about the progress of the undersea war. His captains had certainly proved the value of their rigorous prewar training; their daring and resourcefulness had matched whatever tactics and technical devices the British had come up with. The results were impressive. From September 1939 to September 1940, the U-boats had sunk 440 merchant ships, totaling 2,330,000 tons, and 12 enemy warships.

In 1939, Adolf Hitler introduce a higher class—the Knigh Cross—to the Order of the In Cross, Germany's princip decoration. Hung from a ri bon, the Knight's Cross initia was unadorned. Later, ascen ing grades were created: o leaves, swords, and diamon

Until 1943, the navy based t award on tonnage sunk—a r ported 100,000 tons merited plain Knight's Cross. But as v tories grew rare, almost a successful mission qualified.

Of the 318 Knight's Cross earned by navy men, 145 we to submariners. The most n ed recipient was Otto Kretsc mer (right), who had destroy a quarter of a million tons b fore his boat was sunk in Mar 1941. Rescued by the Allies an imprisoned, Kretschmer, wl already had the Knight's Cro with Oak Leaves, was award the swords to his medal (insi right) in absentia.

In August 1940, Karl Raeder presents the Knight's Cross to Otto Kretschmer, who had sunk 117,000 tons after commanding the U-99 for three months. Oak leaves were added in November, when he reached 200,000 tons.

Yet Dönitz continued to face a nagging numbers problem: He was still short of submarines. He had only fifty-six, the number he had when the war began. (Twenty-eight boats had been sunk and replaced by an equal number of new commissions.) Until July of 1940, he had rarely had enough boats to deploy more than seven or eight at a time. On September 1, 1940, Dönitz had twenty-seven boats available for operations, fewer than he had a year earlier, because he had to detail a larger number for use as trainers. Belatedly, the building program had resumed, with an emphasis on the moderately sized boats that Dönitz wanted. In June, over protests from Raeder and Dönitz, Hitler had confirmed that a maximum of twenty-five new U-boats would be delivered each month. In the second half of 1940, however, only six new boats were commissioned monthly. The figure rose to thirteen in the first six months of 1941 and to twenty the rest of that year but never reached the promised target of twenty-five. As a result, the U-boat command remained far short of the 300 undersea boats that Dönitz insisted he needed to bring Britain to its knees.

The lack of boats caused Dönitz to disagree with Raeder's proposed Mediterranean Plan. In the summer of 1940, Raeder had recommended a bold strategy to capture Gibraltar and Suez, force the British from the Mediterranean, and threaten their supply lines across the South Atlantic and Indian oceans. Such a campaign might wound Britain, Dönitz argued, but could not be decisive because it posed "no direct threat to its island base." Moreover, the German resources, including U-boats, needed to accomplish Raeder's plan would diminish the "already wholly inadequate forces in the decisive theater of operations, the Atlantic."

In November 1940, the first winter storms pounded across the North Atlantic. Winds up to fifty miles per hour pelted men on bridge watch with stinging, icy salt water. Waves, sometimes thirty feet high, broke over the conning tower; to prevent being swept overboard, the submariners lashed themselves to the bridge with safety belts. In such conditions, sighting convoys was impossible. Radio signals from the U-boats to headquarters became terse and to the point: "Operations suspended due to weather."

Adding to the U-boats' problems was the increased number of escort vessels and aircraft that the British had available now that the threat of invasion had been lifted. The extra planes greatly augmented air cover for convoys near the coastline. To avoid confrontation with the Royal Air Force, Dönitz ordered his submarine patrols farther west in the Atlantic. With only four to six boats on patrol at any time and with broader stretches of the ocean to search, locating a convoy became increasingly difficult. During the month of December, only one was sighted.

Plummeting statistics reflected Dönitz's problems. In October, his boats had sunk a record sixty-one ships of 344,513 tons. In November, those figures had slipped to thirty-four ships of 173,995 tons, and in December, thirty-nine ships of 219,501 tons. By Christmas of 1940, only one U-boat was left in the North Atlantic. The euphoria of that golden summer and fall, the Happy Time, had faded. After patrolling for six weeks, many U-boats returned to base, low on fuel, without having fired a torpedo. Their crews—wet, cold, and tired but mostly bored and frustrated by the weeks of unproductive cruising—had plenty of time to ponder the less glamorous realities of life inside their vulnerable little universe.

First and last, the type-VII U-boat was designed to be a weapon—a fast, highly maneuverable torpedo-carrier. Little thought was given to the comfort of the roughly forty-four men who would live for two weeks to two months in a steel tube, 220 feet long and 20 feet at its widest point. When a submarine went to sea, every nook and corner was crammed with precious edibles. Huge smoked hams and sausages hung from the overhead pipes. Sleeping hammocks overflowed with loaves of bread, and sacks of potatoes were stuffed under mess tables. Often, one of the two tiny toilets was turned into a larder, rendering it unusable as a head until the provisions had been consumed.

Wearing oilskins to ward off the searing wind and freezing spray, submariners *(left)* survey the winter horizon for prey. In the cold, guidelines and aerials *(below)* became encrusted with ice, but the U-boat's low center of gravity enabled it to ride out all but the roughest seas.

Privacy was nonexistent; even the captain's quarters were shielded from the rest of the boat by only a curtain. Sleeping accommodations were shared, by officers as well as enlisted men. Crew members coming off their four-hour watch would simply flop, fully clothed, in the hammocks and bunks vacated by the sailors who relieved them or on mattresses strewn across the deck plates. In the perpetual glare of electric lights, day and night blurred into one.

With space so limited, physical exercise was out of the question. Even getting fresh air was a problem for submariners not on watch; two or three people at a time could be allowed on deck briefly, when the weather and operational conditions permitted. Men were sometimes allowed to smoke in the conning tower or on the bridge during the day (never at night, when a cigarette's glow might betray a boat's location). Smoking inside the vessel was prohibited because explosive gases were emitted periodically when the wet batteries were charged.

Two unforgettable characteristics of U-boat life were described by one veteran as "foul air and universal damp." The humidity was close to intolerable. The boats had no heating or air conditioning. Moisture condensed on the cold steel hull and ran in rivulets into the bilges. Clammy clothes never dried out. Food rotted; when loaves of white bread became mildewed, the sailors called them "white rabbits," picked them up by the "ears," and tore out the still-edible insides.

The heavy odor was a blend of many sources: from the bilges; from engine diesel oil; from unwashed bodies (fresh water aboard was strictly for cooking and drinking—the men had to use salt water for washing); from Kolibri, the cologne that crew members coming off watch used to remove crusts of sea salt from their faces; and despite an air purifier, from whatever vapors escaped from behind the door of the overworked head. That particular amenity required careful handling. Because of outside water pressure, the toilet could be flushed only when the boat was within eighty feet of the surface. Valves had to be opened and closed in a specific sequence before the pumping-out operation could begin. And woe to the sailor who got the sequence wrong.

Another chronic condition of life aboard a U-boat was the noise—the hammering of piston engines, the thrashing of propellers—and the ceaseless motion. With each swell, each surge of the waves, the surfaced boat would roll, pitch, yaw, wallow, and shudder. In very heavy seas, a boat would heel to an angle of fifty or sixty degrees, hurling sleeping men out of their bunks to painful landings on the deck below. Even when a U-boat was submerged, it was never still; the slightest transfer of weight, a single

At right, a U-boat enters its protected berth at an occupied French port. The Todt Organization built the massive bunkers, such as the one below at Saint-Nazaire, using workers from Germany and forced French labor. Their roofs of reinforced concrete and corrugated iron withstood Allied bombing until the last days of the war.

man moving forward or aft, could disturb the balance and set the boat swaying.

When a submarine ran on the surface, the chance of a sailor's being swept overboard was a constant risk. On at least thirty occasions during the war, crew members were lost this way. The worst incident occurred in the Bay of Biscay on October 23, 1941, when a surging wave from a following sea washed overboard the entire four-man bridge watch of the U-106. Another constant danger was the possibility that the boat might be sighted by enemy aircraft. But the factor that contributed most to the *Blechkoller,* or tin-can neurosis, was the numbing fear that seized the submariners as they sweated out depth-charge attacks in their submerged vessel. Herbert Werner, a U-boat commander, described the experience. First, he wrote, came "the sharp metallic ping-ping of the asdic impulses that the destroyers sent out to track us down—like a hammer hitting a tuning fork." Then followed the explosions from the first depth charges. "After each shattering roar, the hull moaned, the floor plates jumped, wood splintered, glass disintegrated, food cans flew through the boat. Then all was black for long seconds, until the emergency lighting came on again."

An attack could last for a full day. Hundreds of depth charges might be dropped, each one logged in by a member of the crew. On one boat, the counter used prune pits to keep track. "We sat at our stations, biting our lips and holding our breath," wrote Werner. "Some of the men lay on deck, staring upward. Others sat and stared into an imaginary something. There was no talking, no coughing." If the air in the submerged boat became too foul as the long hours passed, each man was issued a rubber tube to breathe through. It contained a cartridge of potash to filter out the carbon dioxide.

Ultimately, the enemy ships broke off the attack. "One by one, they churned over our coffin," Werner recorded, "each dropping a final depth charge like chrysanthemums upon our grave." The U-boat, if its hull had

held tight under the force of the explosive charges, surfaced once again. "We inhaled the fresh air gratefully, although a sudden abundance of it almost made us black out. The ventilators transported oxygen to the sweating hands inside the drum. For us on the bridge, the sun was never so red nor the sky so blue."

None of the danger or discomfort mattered long if a patrol was successful. Then the submarine glided into home port, proudly flying a victory pennant for each enemy ship it had sunk. Lined up on the quays to greet it were crews from other boats, a band, and pretty nurses from nearby military hospitals offering bouquets of flowers, bottles of champagne, and exuberant kisses. Sometimes Dönitz himself appeared. The U-boat commander in chief, affectionately referred to as *Onkel Karl* or *der Löwe* (the Lion), awarded medals on the spot or simply chatted familiarly with each member of the crew. The sight of his returning heroes never failed to move him. "When I saw them," he later wrote, "emaciated, strained, their pale

The pleasures that waited in port helped to gird submariners' morale during hard times at sea. Here, returning crew members delight in opening the backlog of mail from home, and a comrade *(right)* hugs the comely Red Cross nurse who met his boat.

faces crowned with beards and their leather jackets smeared with oil, there was a tangible bond between us."

Best of all for the men was the shore leave that followed, several weeks usually, before they had to return to sea. Some boarded a special train for Germany and home. Others took advantage of new rest centers at Carnac, Quiberon, and La Baule, called by the men "U-boat pastures." There they could swim, ride horseback, relax, and chase young Frenchwomen. Since the extra allowances for submarine duty almost doubled their regular pay, they could afford fine French foods, wine, and clothes. Even those sailors who had to stay with their boats found plenty of night-clubs and brothels to amuse them during their off-duty hours. U-boat crews usually had their favorite bars. One of them was renowned for a beautiful barmaid named Franziska who would always greet return-ing crewmen: "Bonjour, monsieur. Retour Atlantik? Tommy nix boom boom?"—The Tommies didn't get you?

"The U-boat will achieve far more," Dönitz wrote to Raeder on December 14, 1940, "if, instead of having to hang around for weeks on end, waiting for some victim to run fortuitously into its arms, it can be directed straight to a target that had previously been discovered for it by air reconnaissance. Every arm of the service possesses its own means of reconnaissance—except the U-boats."

For almost two years, Dönitz had operated with practically no air sup-port. Now, in his usual no-nonsense style, he was once again making a pitch for a naval air arm. Raeder, who needed no convincing, sent him to plead his case with General Alfred Jodl, chief of staff of the High Command of the Wehrmacht. Jodl was won over, and on January 7, 1941, while Luftwaffe chief Hermann Göring was off shooting game, Hitler, as Dönitz wryly put it, "broke into the Reich marshal's air force preserve." The Führer placed Group 40, a unit of Condors based at Bordeaux, at Dönitz's disposal.

The planes were a military version of the Focke-Wulf 200 civil airliner. Home from the hunt, Göring, who since prewar days had insisted that "everything that flies belongs to us," was furious at having an air-force unit placed under the command of a navy man. A month later, when Göring's lavishly appointed headquarters train happened to be near Dönitz's command at Kernével, the Reich marshal invited the admiral for a visit. It was the first time the two had met. Göring tried to talk Dönitz into helping him persuade Hitler to rescind the order. Dönitz refused and turned down an invitation to stay for dinner. "We parted," Dönitz recalled, "bad friends."

Dönitz's hope that the reconnaissance planes would help his U-boats home in on targets proved illusory. Only two planes a day—instead of the twelve promised—were available for sorties. Although the Condors had been fitted with extra fuel tanks to allow them to fly from Bordeaux to the main U-boat operational area west and northwest of the North Channel, the planes lacked sufficient capacity to remain there long. If they happened to sight a convoy, they could not maintain contact until the U-boats arrived. The shortage of fuel capacity also prohibited them from returning to France. Instead, they had to fly to an airfield on the west coast of Norway—a dicey proposition because of the chronically foggy conditions there.

Another major problem was the Condors' inaccurate navigational reports, which were sometimes off by as much as eighty miles. At times, after a Condor had allegedly pinpointed the location of a convoy, the wolf pack sent to the spot found only empty ocean. Although daily air reconnaissance did provide a useful general picture of Allied shipping, Dönitz was forced to rely on his U-boats to find targets in the North Atlantic.

Despite the reconnaissance problems, the naval high command remained optimistic. By February of 1941, British ships were going down at the awesome rate of half a million tons a month, three times faster than British and American shipyards could replace them. German strategists had estimated that, if their U-boats, planes, surface ships, and mines combined could destroy 750,000 tons each month, Britain would be forced out of the war within a year. That figure, they felt, was easily attainable if the Luftwaffe alone, as fully expected, could destroy 300,000 tons monthly. But the British lifeline had to be cut soon—before the combined Anglo-American shipbuilding program reached 500,000 tons a month, a goal the Allies would reach sometime in 1942.

In March, the submarine service suffered a grievous blow: Five U-boats and their crews were lost at sea, including three of Dönitz's best commanders. First to set out on that fateful patrol was Günther Prien, who left Lorient aboard the U-47 on February 19. Otto Kretschmer was there to wish his old friend well. "Get a convoy lined up for me, Günther," he teased.

From the deck of the U-47, Lieut. Commander Günther Prien, the hero of Scapa Flow, salutes the crowd assembled to see him off from Lorient in February of 1941. It turned out to be the final patrol for Prien and his boat.

"Just leave it to Papa's nose to smell something out," Prien replied. "I have a hunch about this trip. I have a feeling it will be a big one for us all."

Three days later, piped off by a military band playing "The Kretschmer March," Kretschmer eased out of Lorient in the U-99. The next day, Joachim Schepke followed in the U-100.

On March 6, Prien found a large westbound convoy, under heavy escort, several hundred miles south of Iceland. Around midnight on the next day, he surfaced under cover of a rainsquall to get closer to the convoy. Suddenly, the squall lifted, unveiling the U-47 to the British destroyer *Wolverine*, which immediately attacked. Prien dived. For more than five hours, he tried every trick he knew to shake the destroyer, changing speed, depth, and direction and lying silent for long stretches. Finally, disabled by depth charges, the U-47 limped fifty feet below the surface, emitting telltale bubbles. The *Wolverine* dropped another pattern of ten depth charges across the path of the bubbles. At 5:43 a.m., a tremendous underwater explosion shattered the ocean's surface. Below, an orange light glowed briefly, then faded into nothingness.

Eight days later, on March 16, Schepke's U-100 was pursuing another convoy off Iceland when depth charges damaged its hull, forcing it to surface. The U-100 then became the first boat to be detected at night by shipboard radar. The destroyer *Vanoc* located the submarine and rammed it at full speed. The *Vanoc*'s sharp bow sliced into the conning tower. Schepke, caught on the bridge, was hurled into the sea and drowned. His boat went to the bottom with all but five of its crew.

Earlier that day, Kretschmer and the U-99 had attacked the same convoy. After he had expended all of his torpedoes, he headed home on the surface under cover of darkness. Then the watch officer made a serious mistake.

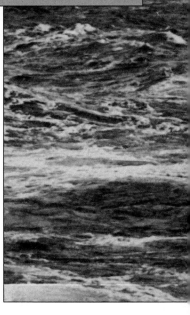

Thinking the U-99 had been sighted by a British destroyer, the *Walker*, he ordered a crash dive to escape, instead of proceeding at full speed on the surface. Once underwater, the U-boat was detected by the destroyer's asdic. Within minutes, depth charges crippled the boat's engines and propellers. At 720 feet, a perilous depth, its hull began to break up. Kretschmer's only choice was to bring his boat rapidly to the surface. Then, as the U-99 listed helplessly in the North Atlantic swell, the skipper calmly smoked a cigar and supervised its scuttling. He and his entire crew jumped into the frigid waters, were quickly picked up, and became prisoners of war.

The loss of Prien, thirty-three years old, and Schepke and Kretschmer, both only twenty-nine, shocked the U-boat command. How could these aggressive, highly experienced captains, who among them had sunk 111 ships totaling 586,694 tons, be hunted down and defeated in a mere eight days? Did the British possess some new antisubmarine weapon?

To buttress the notion of U-boat invincibility, Germany until now had never publicly acknowledged the loss of a submarine. Members of the U-boat command knew about earlier losses as they occurred, of course, but civilians were given no reason to doubt the invulnerability of the U-boats. Worried about the effect on morale the dramatic loss of three of the Reich's military idols might cause, Hitler ordered that no public announcement be made. The news of Prien's death was kept even from his wife (whose mauve scarf he had always worn around his neck on patrol). Not until the end of April were the fates of Schepke and Kretschmer revealed, and Prien's loss was not made public until May 23, ten weeks after his death.

For Dönitz, the loss of the three commanders was personal and devastating. Schepke, he wrote, had been a "real thruster"; Kretschmer, "quick in sizing up a situation and in realizing best how to exploit it." But Prien had been special—"all that a man should be, a great personality, full of zest and energy and the joy of life, wholly dedicated to his service."

In an order of the day announcing the death of his favorite, Admiral Dönitz made the following defiant pledge to his command: "Günther Prien, the hero of Scapa Flow, has made his last patrol. We submariners bow our heads with pride and sorrow. Even though the vast ocean hides him, Prien

The sound of a destroyer such as HMS *Walpole (above)* pursuing an asdic contact struck fear into the hearts of submariners. But at close range, the asdic's sound waves missed the U-boat; sailors launching depth charges *(above, left)* could only guess the location of their quarry and had to watch the explosions *(right)* for debris or other evidence of a hit.

still stands in our midst. No U-boat will go to sea against the West, but he will sail with it. No blow against England will be struck by us, but his aggressive spirit will guide our hand."

Although Dönitz and his staff were not aware that the destroyer *Vanoc* had used a new radar system to spot Schepke's U-100, they nevertheless suspected that the loss of the three boats might have been more than simple coincidence. Dönitz ordered all his boats away from the area south of Iceland where they had been operating. But when, in March and April, his boats sank eighty-four ships totaling more than 492,395 tons, he decided that the trumping of his three aces had been "purely fortuitous" and not the result of any new enemy technique or secret weapon.

Indeed, Great Britain's antisubmarine defense had improved so gradually up to that time that it had never really threatened Germany's U-boat operations. In early 1941, planes of the Coastal Command and some escort vessels had been outfitted with a new radar set of RAF design that was smaller and more sophisticated than its predecessor. In theory, the radar would enable escort vessels to locate surfaced U-boats at night before they could attack. In practice, however, until wavelengths and directional aerials were modified, the radar proved more useful in helping ships maintain their positions in convoys when visibility was poor than in locating U-boats in time to do any good.

More significant was the marked increase in convoy escorts. As the threat of German invasion receded, more and more British ships—as well as the fifty aged destroyers that President Franklin D. Roosevelt had traded to Churchill—were allocated to escort duty. The fleet of roughly 235 escorts available in July 1940 swelled to about 375, including 240 destroyers, by the following March. The increase not only provided more protection for the merchantmen but enabled the British to start training convoy escort groups to operate as coordinated teams.

The German high command had never believed that radar would play an important role in the war. Faced with fiercely competing demands on Germany's resources, Hitler in 1941 had ordered the abandonment of any research into radar improvements that could not be completed within one year. Meanwhile, the British had reported the first radar-assisted attack against a U-boat as early as November 1940. In February 1941, they claimed to have sunk a U-boat that they had located by radar from the air. In the first instance, the U-boat escaped; in the second, the U-boat command had no record of a loss that month. In any case, because the British were not yet using radar on a large scale, Dönitz and his staff regarded such incidents as ordinary attacks. Even later in the year, when U-boat commanders began reporting that they had been surprised by unexpected air attacks, staff officers at Dönitz's headquarters simply shrugged off the reports. "The lookouts," they rationalized, "were not awake." Not until 1942 did a ranking officer suggest that the real explanation may have been improvements in British radio-ranging techniques.

The Germans knew, of course, that the British were monitoring radio traffic to and from U-boat command headquarters and the boats at sea, as well as between individual submarines on patrol. They did not suspect that the enemy had broken their secret codes. But even uncoded radio traffic might provide enough information for the British to divert some convoys from steaming into the wolf packs' lair.

HMS *Rajputana* sinks in the Denmark Strait after Lieut. Commander Klaus Scholtz's U-108 torpedoed it in April of 1941. Dönitz had sent Scholtz to the passage between Greenland and Iceland with orders to find and sink the auxiliary cruiser, which had been reporting on German naval activity in the area.

In fact, the British direction-finding (D-F) network, reaching from the Shetland Islands to Land's End, was already providing excellent coverage of German radio communications originating east of the United Kingdom. Once new D-F stations were established in Iceland, Greenland, and Newfoundland, the network blanketed the entire North Atlantic. Dönitz had to assume that every radio signal broadcast by a U-boat at sea would be picked up and eventually give away the boat's position. He could not, of course, ban the use of radio; his entire method of operation—finding targets and deploying his submarines in packs to attack them—depended on radio communication. Instead, he ordered his captains to limit their radio traffic in the future to absolutely essential communication and to frequently change wavelengths and bands to make it more difficult for British D-F stations to pick them up.

More worrisome than D-F was the problem that had plagued Dönitz from the start: not enough submarines to find targets in the broad Atlantic. Complicating that task was the continuing policy of the naval high command to take boats away from him for what he considered to be "sideshows." Two U-boats had to be stationed at all times in the western Atlantic to provide weather reports for Göring's Luftwaffe. When Hitler invaded the Soviet Union in June 1941, Dönitz received orders to send eight boats to the Baltic. They found virtually nothing there to shoot at and were returned to him in September. From July onward, he had to detach another four to six boats for operations in the Arctic, an exercise in futility because Allied convoys had not yet begun to carry supplies to Russia's Barents Sea ports. And time and again, U-boats were diverted from their attack role in order to serve as escorts for blockade runners, auxiliary cruisers, supply ships, and captured prize vessels.

Following the air Battle of Britain, a weakened Luftwaffe factored less and less in the continual battle for control of the Atlantic. Only once, in April 1941, had the air force come close to sinking 300,000 tons of Allied shipping, its projected monthly target. Dönitz became more convinced than ever that his U-boats would have to be the dominant weapon if economic strangulation were to force Britain to surrender. He could not argue personally with Hitler about sideshows, of course. But each time a decision was about to be made that could harm his operations, he could and did take his case to Raeder and the naval high command. Most of the time, Raeder agreed with Dönitz and pressed his arguments on the Führer.

Sometimes Dönitz's messianic zeal was too much even for Raeder and his staff. Once he complained that 800 dockyard workers had been withdrawn from working on his submarines to repair the damaged cruiser *Hipper.* (The U-boats already had to spend sixty-five days in drydock for each thirty-five at sea because of a shortage of yard workers.) One of Raeder's staff officers returned Dönitz's long memorandum on the subject with the marginal comment, "We don't want to become a navy of U-boats."

Dönitz based his unwavering advocacy on simple arithmetic: U-boats, he felt, should be sent on missions outside the North Atlantic only when the potential for sinking enemy tonnage elsewhere made it worthwhile. In June 1940, under pressure from the naval high command to diversify his operations, he had reluctantly agreed to send one boat into the South Atlantic, and in the next six months he dispatched two more. Only in February 1941, when the "effective U-boat quotient" in the north had gone down, did he begin to send newly commissioned type-IX submarines into the South Atlantic off Freetown, Sierra Leone, on the west coast of Africa. Freetown, 2,800 miles from the German bases on the Bay of Biscay, was the assembly point for Allied shipping coming from South America and around the Cape of Good Hope from the Middle and Far East. Relatively slow ships formed convoys there; faster vessels sailed north independently. Although the type-IX boats were bigger and clumsier than the VIIs, they had greater range. By rendezvousing in secret with surface supply ships to take on fuel and torpedoes, they could conduct two patrols before returning to base. And the pickings were good off Freetown: The big boats destroyed seventy-four enemy ships. One submarine, the U-107 commanded by Lieut. Commander Günther Hessler, sank fourteen merchantmen totaling 87,000 tons, the most successful U-boat cruise of the war. "A remarkable performance," Dönitz commented, "even for a man who is an excellent tactician and a master in the art of the use of the torpedo." Hessler also was Dönitz's son-in-law, a fact that made Dönitz reluctant to recommend him for the Knight's Cross; he feared that critics might charge favoritism. Dönitz relented only when Raeder told him in exasperation that he would recommend Hessler for the medal if Dönitz did not.

By the spring of 1941, it was obvious to Dönitz that the increasingly blatant role of the U.S. Navy in protecting Britain's Atlantic lifeline would sooner or later lead to clashes between neutral American ships and German U-boats. On June 20, the U-203, patrolling the blockade zone around the British Isles in which Hitler had given German submarines unrestricted permission to attack, sighted the USS *Texas*, a battleship. It was the first time an American warship had ventured inside the zone—an incursion the Führer had not anticipated when he issued the order. The U-boat captain reported the sighting to headquarters and, without waiting for a reply, tried to get into position to fire his torpedoes. But heavy seas and the battleship's zigzag course foiled the attack. Dönitz ordered the U-203 to break off the encounter, and the following day, after checking with Hitler, he sent the following message to all his boats: "Führer orders avoidance of any incident with USA during next few weeks. Order will be rigidly obeyed in all circumstances. In addition, attacks until further orders will be restricted to cruisers, battleships, and aircraft carriers and then only when identified beyond doubt as hostile. Fact that warship is sailing without lights will not be regarded as proof of enemy identity."

By bending over backward to avoid any incident that might provide the

United States with an excuse for entering the war, Hitler had muzzled Dönitz's gray wolves. With American warships now intermingled with British ships on convoy duty, the U-boats could no longer attack even their most dangerous foes—the British destroyers, frigates, and corvettes—for fear of sinking an American ship by accident. (A later order permitted U-boats to defend themselves—but only against attacks in progress.) Dönitz, who was aware of the political reasons behind the Führer's orders, accepted them with relatively good grace, but his commanders and crews became angry and frustrated.

Further run-ins between U-boats and American ships were inevitable. On September 4, 1941, south of Iceland, the U-652 was depth-charged by a British plane and retaliated by firing two torpedoes at a pursuing destroyer, which turned out to be the USS *Greer*. The torpedoes missed. On October 10, a torpedo from an attacking U-boat struck the USS *Kearney*, a destroyer escorting a British convoy, and eleven members of its crew were killed. They were the first American military casualties of the war. Three weeks later, in the frigid waters southwest of Iceland, the U-552, commanded by twenty-seven-year-old Erich Topp, approached what he believed was a British convoy escorted by British destroyers. But the ship in his cross hairs was the American destroyer *Reuben James*. In an interview many years later, Topp described the encounter. "We attacked at dawn with two torpedoes," he recalled. "One hit amidships and detonated normally. A

As an officer *(left)* photographs the kill, Lieut. Commander Günther Hessler watches a torpedoed steamer sink off Freetown, Sierra Leone. The ship was one of a record fourteen that Hessler's U-107 sank during a three-month-long patrol in 1941. Survivors in lifeboats *(above)* were pulled alongside the U-boat, given provisions, and directed toward the nearest land. Those in need of medical aid, such as the sailor prostrate on the deck at right, were treated and returned to the lifeboats.

short time later, a terrible second detonation just about atomized the destroyer. We found out eventually that it was carrying depth charges that had already been primed, and they exploded, too. The feeling at such a moment is that we had fought and sunk our enemy, and destroyers were our worst enemy," Topp said. "Later, the memory gave me many sleepless nights."

One hundred fifteen American officers and enlisted men went down with the *Reuben James.* The sinking, more than a month before Pearl Harbor, became an emotional rallying cry for those who wanted the United States to enter the war against Hitler's Germany.

At the same time, the performance charts in the Museum at U-boat headquarters in Kernével, France, were becoming less reassuring. From a total of 635,635 tons of shipping sunk in May and June, the amount plummeted to 174,519 tons in July and August. During the month of August, nearly one million tons of imports reached Great Britain each week, the highest figure of the year.

By early autumn, Dönitz was ready to step up the offensive. He now had almost 200 boats, approximately 80 of them in action at any one time. But events on a distant front conspired against him. Since early summer, General Erwin Rommel had beseeched Hitler for aid in supplying his Afrikakorps. Deeply worried over the Allied threat to Rommel's lifeline, the Führer, with the concurrence of the naval high command, ordered the U-boat fleet to shift its primary operations to the Strait of Gibraltar and the Mediterranean. Dönitz protested vehemently, to no avail. U-boat warfare in the North Atlantic came to a virtual halt. In November, only eighteen enemy ships were sunk, and in December only twelve, for a two-month total of less than 154,000 tons.

Several other factors contributed to the slowdown, although Dönitz was not aware of them. On May 9, the U-110, commanded on its second patrol by the now-famous Fritz-Julius Lemp, attacked a heavily escorted convoy off the southern tip of Greenland and was forced to the surface by a British corvette. Fearing that they were about to be rammed, Lemp and most of his crew abandoned ship after setting delayed explosive charges to scuttle the submarine. When Lemp realized that the charges had not gone off and that the British were about to take the vessel, he tried to climb back to reset the charges, but a member of the boarding party shot him dead. The British captured the U-110 intact, including all its code books, cipher documents, and the so-called Enigma machine used to encipher radio messages.

The dramatic exploit reaped immediate rewards. Working around the clock, British cryptographers broke the main operational cipher, code-named *Heimisch*, or Home. Within a week, they were deciphering German radio traffic and directing convoy commanders to change course. From June to August, U-boats intercepted only four percent of Allied convoys in the North Atlantic, and from September to December, only eighteen percent.

The British kept secret the capture of the U-110. Dönitz, failing to hear from the submarine by radio, simply assumed that it had been sunk or scuttled and was unaware that he had lost his communications security. He also did not know about another British coup at sea: the capture intact on August 28, 1941, of the U-570, eighty miles south of Iceland. While surfacing, the submarine was spied by a British aircraft, which swooped down to attack. The U-boat captain, on his first patrol, panicked and waved his white shirt in surrender. The U-570 provided British experts with a good deal of information about a U-boat's speed, its maneuvering characteristics, its diving capabilities, and the character and volume of the various noises its machinery made—vital data to antisubmarine tacticians. Once the investigators were done with it, the U-570 was renamed HMS *Graph* and sent back to sea with a British crew.

In October, British defensive capabilities were boosted further when new high-frequency direction finders were installed at coastal stations and aboard convoy escorts. Called Huff-Duff by British sailors, the electronic detection device could tune in on radio messages that a U-boat at sea sent to Dönitz's headquarters on land and, after the German boat had broadcast as few as four digits, could zero in on its location. An entire convoy needed

The capture of the German submarine U 570 by a Lockheed "Hudson" of the British Coastal Command.

BACK THEM UP!

A British poster portrays the surrender of the U-570 to a Coastal Command reconnaissance plane that had dropped depth charges on the submarine as it surfaced off Iceland in August 1941. The American-built Lockheed Hudson circled the U-boat for hours until the Royal Navy towed the prize to port.

only one Huff-Duff to warn it of approaching U-boats. Despite German intelligence photographs showing Huff-Duff antennas aboard escort ships and indiscreet references to the new device made in Allied ship-to-ship radio conversation, Dönitz and his staff apparently never caught on to its existence aboard ships.

Before the year ended, Dönitz was to suffer one more hammer blow. He assembled a pack of nine U-boats to attack a convoy, designated HG76, of thirty-two merchantmen that sailed from Gibraltar on December 14, a week after Pearl Harbor. The convoy had an exceptionally strong escort—one destroyer, seven corvettes, two sloops, and, for the first time, an auxiliary aircraft carrier, the *Audacity*. Supplementing the carrier's six planes were shore-based aircraft, first from Gibraltar and later from England, that provided an almost-continuous air umbrella.

The Enigma ciphering machines used by the submarine command to communicate with its boats resembled a typewriter set in a wooden box. Rotating wheels—three in this model—scrambled the typed message in a nearly infinite combination of letters.

Dönitz's raiders intercepted the convoy off the coast of Spain and dogged it northward, day after day. But after a week, the submarines had managed to sink only the *Audacity*, the destroyer *Stanley*, and two of the thirty-two merchantmen. Surface ships and aircraft pursued the U-boats relentlessly. (One boat had to dive for its life eight times in nineteen hours.) Five U-boats were sunk, one of them commanded by Lieut. Commander Engelbert Endrass, who had become Dönitz's reigning ace. When an American-made Liberator bomber, which had flown 800 miles from its base in England, appeared over the convoy on December 22, Dönitz ordered the four surviving wolves to break off the fight. Licking their wounds, they limped home.

The standoff with HG76 and the meager results of the previous two months led some on Dönitz's staff to suggest that U-boats could no longer successfully attack convoys. Although Dönitz had written earlier in his war diary that "the presence of aircraft makes wolf-pack tactics impossible," he refused to give in to pessimism. He did, however, broadcast a new directive. Until now, a U-boat captain's first responsibility when he sighted a convoy had been not to attack but simply to maintain contact until other boats could be sent to the area. Dönitz now granted his commanders discretionary power to attack any aircraft carrier escorting a convoy without first reporting back and waiting for support. Clearly, the odds favoring the hunter over the hunted had narrowed. "The year 1941 came to an end," Dönitz wrote, "in an atmosphere of worry and anxiety." ✚

Comrades in Cramped Quarters

1 Preparing for sea, U-boat crew members patiently pass books through their boat's galley hatch. Provisioning was tedious: All supplies, from food and clothing to oxygen tanks and spare-time reading, were handed aboard through the narrow hatches.

2 A crewman carries an armload of the hard, dark navy bread called *Kommissbrot.* A U-boat typically went on patrol with about four tons of food—enough to feed fifty men for two months.

3 Supervised by the submarine's watch officer *(center, rear),* torpedomen strain to maneuver a 1.5-ton torpedo through the U-59's forward torpedo hatch at the dock in Lorient.

The first time I stepped into that claustrophobic narrowness, I thought, 'You can't stand this,'" recalled U-boat commander Erich Topp of his introduction to the cramped, malodorous world of submarines. Service aboard a U-boat was a far cry from the glamorous adventure advertised to the German public. Yet most of the young sea wolves, including Topp, adapted to life within their aptly nicknamed iron coffins; those who survived one patrol could scarcely wait for the next.

Isolated for months at a time and always at risk, a U-boat crew came to function as if it were a single organism. Each man grew acutely aware of the other's thoughts and foibles, and all were intimately tuned to the sea around them. "A U-boat molds the people on board," said Topp, who became Germany's third highest scoring naval ace. "The sea becomes a natural part of their lives, and they develop new senses, senses that react to noises, vibrations, salt, water, and the layers of temperature in the sea. When a U-boat man leaves port and closes the hatch in the tower, he says good-bye to the world of color, the sun, the moon, the stars, and the diverse beauty of the earth. His life in the steel tube is reduced to a few principles, of which the most important are companionship and the will to survive."

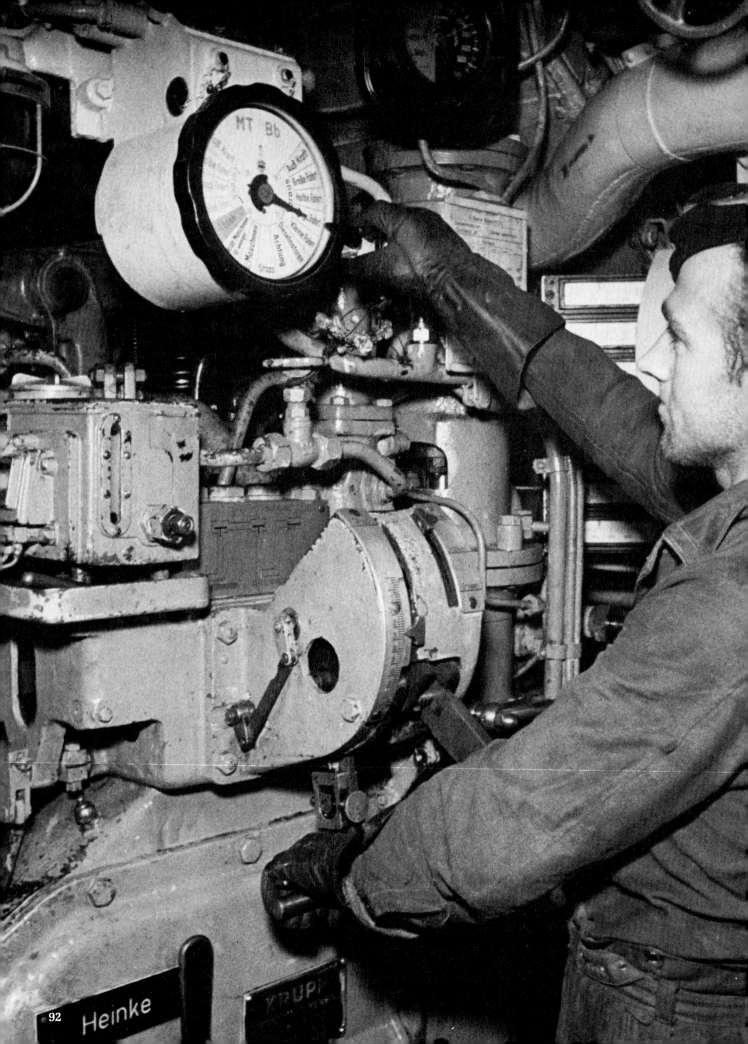

Heinke

An Able
Hand at
Every Post

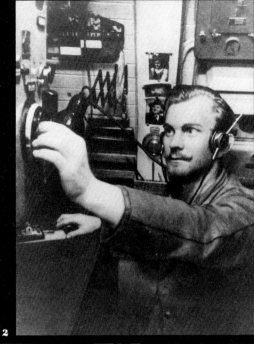

2

3

4

1   A diesel-room machinist, wear-
    ing gloves to protect his skin
    from hot engine parts, grips the
    boat's manual control throttle
    with his left hand. He moves the
    telegraph dial pointer with his
    right, automatically signaling
    that he has received the
    captain's order to change speed.

2   The radio operator listens for
    incoming signals on his long-
    wave receiver, the submarine's
    link to the outside world. Long
    waves could penetrate about
    thirty feet of water, reaching a
    submerged U-boat's antenna
    when the boat was as much as
    seventy feet beneath the surface.

3   Heinrich Lehmann-Willenbrock,
    the captain of the U-96, peers
    through the navigation periscope
    in his control room. He wears
    the white cap cover adopted
    on many U-boats as the badge
    of the commanding officer.

4   Torpedomen carefully adjust the
    guidance system on one of their
    undersea missiles as part of
    the constant checking of the
    torpedoes' batteries, propellants,
    and firing mechanisms.

Making the Best
of Undersea
Fare

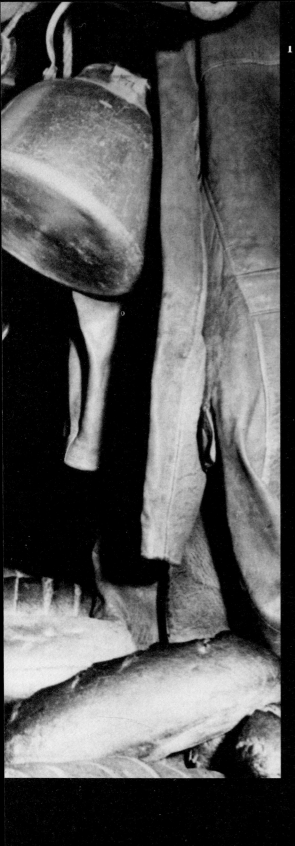

1

1 As a patrol begins, members of the crew take inventory of provisions, including sausages suspended overhead in the forward torpedo compartment. The U-boats had no food lockers, and edibles, while they lasted, filled every spare inch of space.

2 A cook samples a pot of soup in his tiny galley. Submariners received the best rations in Germany's armed forces, but the food quickly took on a distinctive taste described by one sailor as "diesel oil flavored with mold."

3 Hunched over a makeshift table-top that rests on two torpedoes, sailors on the U-103 concentrate on downing a hot meal.

Fighting Fatigue and Perpetual Damp

1 A submariner spreads his sweaters and socks to dry over a U-boat's motor control panel. Despite such efforts, most clothing remained perpetually damp in the boats' humid air.

2 Oblivious to their surroundings, two off-duty sailors concentrate on a game of chess. To boost morale, commanders encouraged chess matches and card tournaments and awarded prizes. They often volunteered to stand the winner's watch.

3 A basin anchored to two torpedo tubes provides a submariner with a seawater sponge bath. Lacking fresh water for bathing, most U-boat men cleaned themselves with Kolibri cologne that contributed a cloying aroma to the already-reeking air.

4 Lying snug in his hammock in a torpedo room, an off-duty machinist passes the time reading.

5 Exhausted crewmen slump between diesel engines to catch a few moments of sleep. Peaceful repose was unknown aboard a U-boat; the men slept in four-hour shifts disrupted by constant light, noise, and the violent pitching of their small craft.

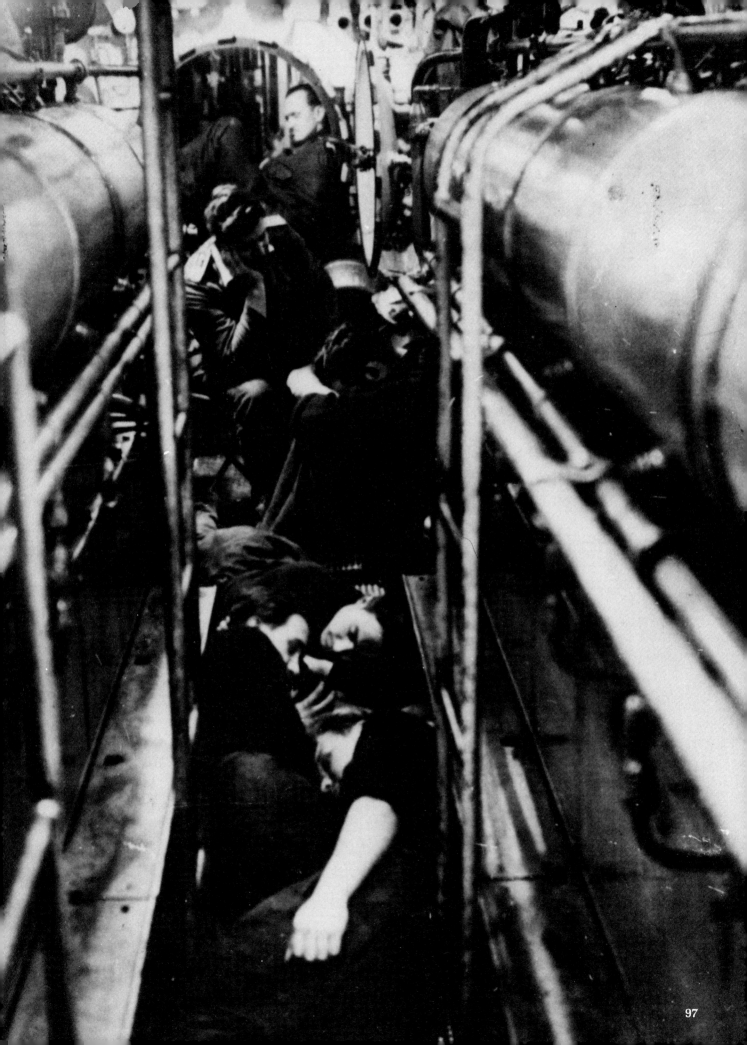

Vulnerable Moments on Deck

2

3

4

A wave sweeps the deck of the U-103 as two crew members make emergency repairs to the boat's 37-mm antiaircraft gun.

White water pours through the U-boat's conning-tower hatch, drenching the crew member who opened it as the submarine surfaced in rough weather.

The bridge crew watches as a flagman signals a passing ship to stop and identify itself. The picture was taken early in the war, when most U-boats fired only after allowing crews of enemy vessels to abandon ship.

Standing precariously on top of the deck gun, a radio operator repairs his boat's antenna with the help of a comrade. Both submariners are tethered to the conning tower by cables clipped to their safety belts.

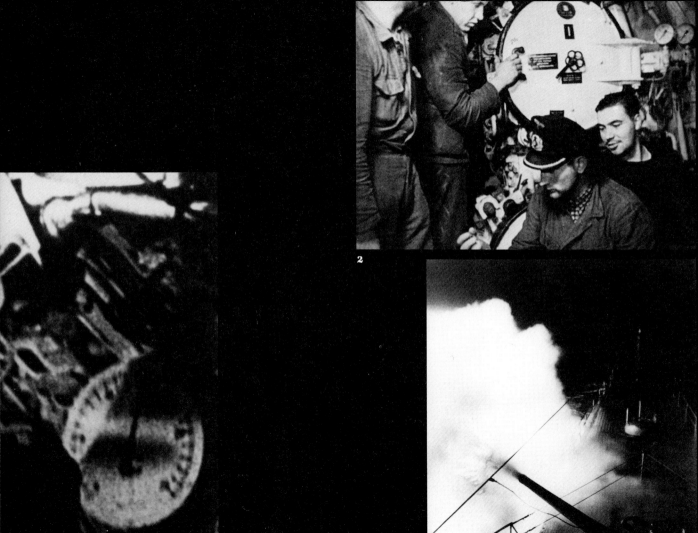

2

Tense Hours
under
Attack

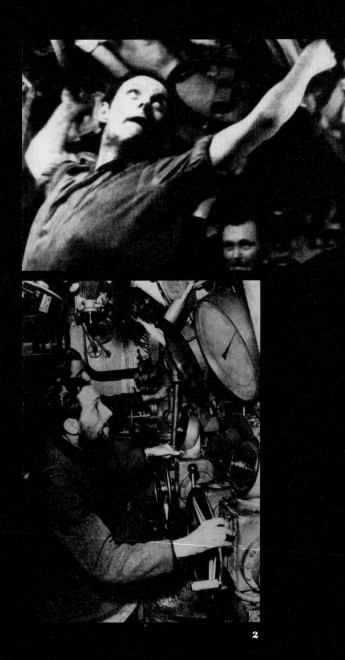

1

2

1 A crew member responds to the
   command to dive by closing one
   of the two main exhaust valves.

2 As his boat dives to evade an
   attack, the captain carefully
   monitors the depth meter. A submarine that ventured too deep
   risked having its valves burst and
   its hull collapse under the
   mounting pressure of the water.

3 Playing possum to deceive a
   destroyer, crew members wear
   felt shoes to muffle their foot-
   steps and pump the bilges by
   hand so the motorized pumps do
   not give them away. Long hours
   of the deadly game have depleted
   the oxygen, so the men breathe
   through carbon dioxide filters.

3

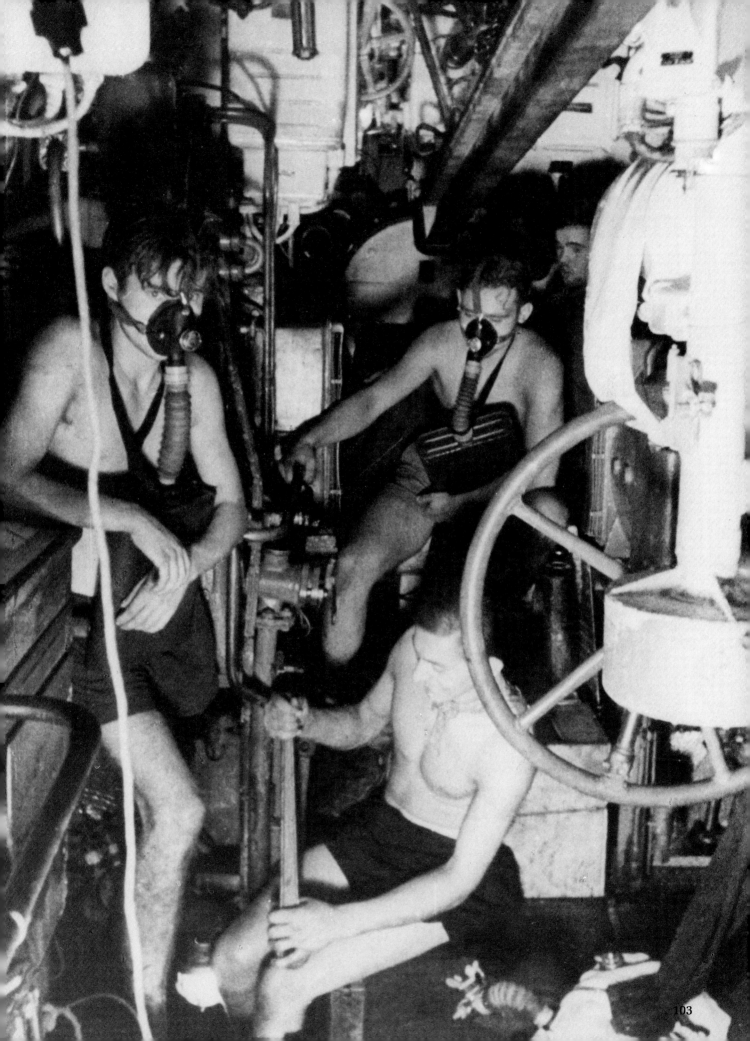

Expanding the Killing Ground

Unterseeboot-81 was about to enter the Mousetrap. No one aboard was deceived by the tranquillity of the fair night skies, the gentle seas, and the balmy air as the submarine cruised on the surface off the coast of Morocco in November 1941. The U-81 and its crew, led by Lieut. Commander Friedrich Guggenberger, were veterans of the submarine war off Murmansk and in the Atlantic, and they knew they were facing one of their most perilous ventures. They intended to penetrate the Strait of Gibraltar.

Admiral Karl Dönitz had summed up his feelings about the dangers of the Mediterranean Sea for U-boats by branding it a mousetrap. On this night, the men of the U-81 were to learn why these waters were the despair of submariners. The passage through the Strait was not only narrow—eight miles across at Tarifa, on the coast of Spain—but shallow and ripped by a west-to-east current that made entrance to the sea fast but exit nearly impossible for a submerged boat. Any U-boat also had to cope with British antisubmarine forces based at Gibraltar. They included the aircraft carrier *Ark Royal*, a battle cruiser, two battleships, and eleven destroyers, all of which defended against such intruders as the U-81.

As midnight approached, the U-81 crept toward the Strait from the southwest, the least likely avenue of approach for a German vessel. When the navigator of the second watch reported on deck, he could smell land and see the lights of Tangier to starboard. "Damned close," he muttered. But by hugging the African coast, the U-81 had already eluded the outer ring of British patrols. As the channel narrowed, the captain steered for the middle, and soon the men topside glimpsed the lights of Tarifa to port. The lookouts, scanning the night with their glasses, spied a large freighter sneaking out to sea with all lights extinguished. It was an inviting target, but this was not the time to attack.

The U-boat kept to the center of the Strait, but to the tense crew it seemed the shores on either side lay only a stone's throw away. Each revolution of the Tarifa lighthouse beacon bathed the submarine's deck with light. The port passed abeam, the Strait began to widen, and across Algeciras Bay the

Smoke boils up from the tanker *Byron T. Benson* after it took a torpedo amidships off Cape Hatteras in April 1942. Between January and July, immediately after the United States had entered the war, a handful of U-boats sank 495 ships in American and Caribbean waters.

fortress rock loomed jagged against the dark sky. Now the lookouts spotted a line of picket boats stretched across the entire width of the Strait. Guggenberger, knowing that the boats might be linked by barriers of nets or cables, stayed on the surface, headed for the widest interval he could see, and hoped for the best. The lights of the picket boats came closer, then abeam. The crew waited in silence for hell to erupt, but the line of lights slid astern. The submariners' luck had held, but they would need more.

Two enemy destroyers appeared ahead, crisscrossing back and forth across the Strait. Guggenberger steered for the point at which the two had just met before they steamed off in opposite directions. The U-81 eased past undetected, safely into the Mediterranean at last. The crew relaxed, and all who were not needed turned in. As the second officer said with a sardonic laugh, "God grant you deep, refreshing sleep, gentlemen."

Repose on a German submarine in those waters could not last long, however. Despite Dönitz's reservations about the usefulness of U-boats here, Hitler in September had ordered six boats to leave their Atlantic hunting grounds and sail to the Mediterranean to help avert an impending disaster in North Africa. In November, the Führer had insisted that four more, including the U-81, join them. Their assignment was not to lie in wait for unarmed merchant ships, but to challenge the might of the Royal Navy.

The fall of France and the declaration of war by Italy in June 1940 had effectively closed the Mediterranean to British shipping from the east. Merchantmen bound for England had to sail around South Africa's Cape of Good Hope. Yet Winston Churchill was determined not to abandon any of the Mediterranean to the enemy. He committed half of Britain's capital ships and thirty-three destroyers to the continuing defense of three British strongpoints—Gibraltar, at the western entrance; the island redoubt of Malta, south of Sicily; and Alexandria, Egypt, near the Suez Canal.

The wisdom of the strategy soon became apparent. The Italians attacked in North Africa in September 1940—striking eastward from Libya toward Alexandria—and invaded Greece in October. Their naval support, however, was woefully outclassed by the powerful British flotilla. Not only did the Italians fail to take Greece, but the British occupied the strategic island of Crete. And in December, well-supplied British forces counterattacked in North Africa, chasing the Italians back toward Libya.

Early in 1941, the Germans came to the Italians' aid. They did so reluctantly, because Hitler was intent on much larger game, an invasion of Russia. But the situation in North Africa and the Balkans had to be stabilized first. In February, Lieut. General Erwin Rommel took two divisions to North Africa to bolster the Italians there, and although his orders were merely to hold his ground, on March 31 he attacked, driving rapidly to the

Lifelines across the Mediterranean

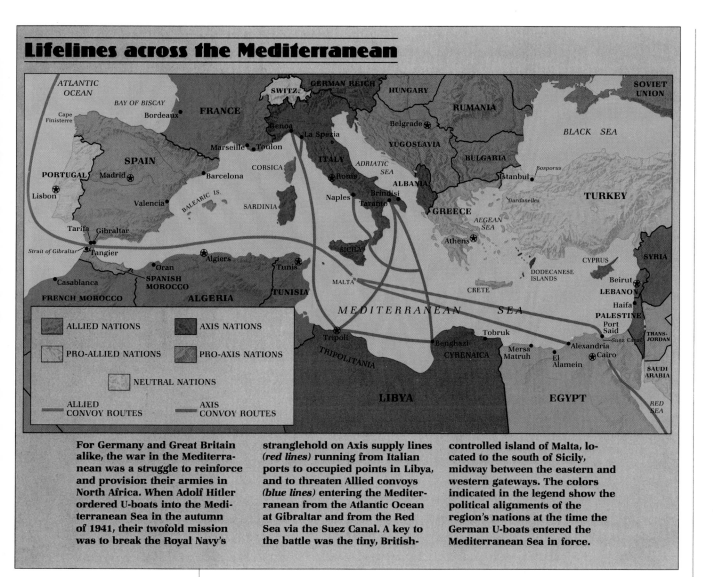

For Germany and Great Britain alike, the war in the Mediterranean was a struggle to reinforce and provision their armies in North Africa. When Adolf Hitler ordered U-boats into the Mediterranean Sea in the autumn of 1941, their twofold mission was to break the Royal Navy's stranglehold on Axis supply lines (*red lines*) running from Italian ports to occupied points in Libya, and to threaten Allied convoys (*blue lines*) entering the Mediterranean from the Atlantic Ocean at Gibraltar and from the Red Sea via the Suez Canal. A key to the battle was the tiny, British-controlled island of Malta, located to the south of Sicily, midway between the eastern and western gateways. The colors indicated in the legend show the political alignments of the region's nations at the time the German U-boats entered the Mediterranean Sea in force.

Egyptian border against British forces that had been weakened in order to reinforce those in Greece. In April, the German army attacked in Greece as well and, in ten days, had the British there against the ropes.

Despite these setbacks, the British averted disaster—entirely because of their navy. British warships continued to harass Italian and German convoys supplying Rommel and bombarded his supply depot at Tripoli with devastating effect. Meanwhile, British vessels supported the friendly fortress at Tobruk, on the Libyan coast seventy-five miles west of Egypt, so staunchly that Rommel had to pass it by, leaving it to further threaten his line of supply. And when the British finally had to abandon Greece at the end of April, their ships successfully evacuated 50,000 soldiers.

Throughout the summer and fall of 1941, meeting only token opposition from the decimated and demoralized Italian fleet, British ships tightened a stranglehold on Rommel's supplies. By September, when Hitler ordered the U-boats into the Mediterranean, one-third of the matériel shipped to Rommel was being sunk or damaged en route. In succeeding months, more than half was lost. Rommel had to retreat almost to where he had started, defeated not only in combat but by logistics. Something had to be done, and Hitler insisted that the U-boats do it.

On November 13, the day following its harrowing entry into the Mediterranean, the U-81 got its chance. U-boat command reported by radio that a British battle group, including the carriers *Ark Royal* and *Furious* and the battleship *Malaya*, had attacked an Italian convoy five hours earlier and then headed west. Guggenberger did not know where the British ships were, but he guessed where they were going—Gibraltar. He brought his boat about and headed back toward the jaws of the trap he had just eluded. To make better time, he ran on the surface, but enemy aircraft and destroyers forced him to dive again and again. Still, he had guessed well. At 2:20 p.m., the three capital ships loomed in his periscope.

Ignoring a screen of six British destroyers and a plane overhead, Guggenberger positioned his submerged boat and readied all four forward torpedo tubes. When the periscope's cross hairs were on the bow of one of the warships, Guggenberger barked the order to fire—"Los!" Because of the sudden loss of weight, the submarine's bow rose ten feet and threatened to break the surface. Guggenberger ordered all hands forward to provide ballast; the bow tilted down, and he ordered a crash dive to 300 feet.

As the U-81 knifed toward the hoped-for safety of deep water, the crew heard the distant thuds of two torpedoes striking home, followed by the churning screws of approaching destroyers. A few depth charges exploded, comfortably wide. Then the sounds on the surface stopped.

Asdic pulses pinged on the hull so loudly the entire crew could hear

A Royal Navy task force led by the aircraft carrier *Ark Royal* steams through the placid waters of the Mediterranean Sea in November of 1940. One year later, the German U-81 sank the 22,000-ton ship off Gibraltar.

U-boat aces Friedrich Guggenberger (*left*) and Hans-Diedrich Freiherr von Tiesenhausen (*right*) chat with Valerio Borghese, an Italian submarine captain, after the three officers received medals for valor from the Italian government in 1942. Guggenberger was honored for sinking the *Ark Royal* (*above*).

them, and knew what they meant. The next sounds were splashes overhead—a broad carpet of depth charges hitting the surface of the water above them. Guggenberger ordered both engines full ahead. The boat had to get out of there. He counted the seconds, knowing that each one brought the depth charges ten feet closer. The helmsman began to stuff prunes into his mouth. The first explosion came at a depth well over 150 feet. The boat flexed and groaned. Light bulbs popped from their sockets. Glass instruments shattered. With each awesome concussion, the helmsman spat a prune pit, his method of keeping score. The destroyers attacked relentlessly, but the U-81 held up against the pressure and slowly eased away from its enemies. After three hours of running, the beleaguered submarine crew heard a depth charge explode two and a half miles away. It turned out to be the last one. The helmsman had long since given up counting with prune pits—to complete his tally, he would have had to eat 130 prunes.

Guggenberger did not know until later that one of his torpedoes had hit the *Ark Royal* with fatal results. Severely damaged, the carrier was being towed to Gibraltar when it sank. Only one man was killed, but seventy-two aircraft were lost. The second torpedo had struck the *Malaya*. It managed to reach Gibraltar but required extensive repairs.

On November 25, twelve days after the U-81's successful attack, Lieutenant Hans-Diedrich Freiherr von Tiesenhausen, commanding the U-331 off the border of Egypt and Libya in the eastern Mediterranean, spotted a

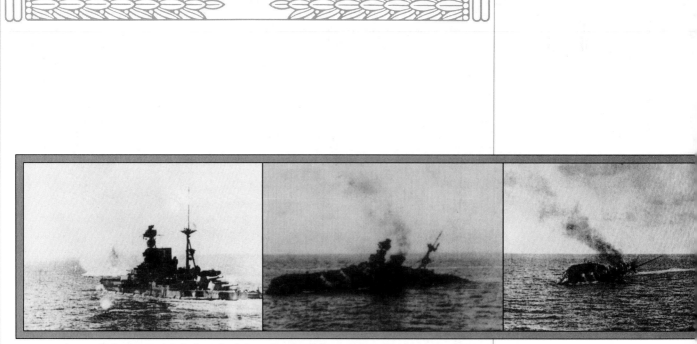

procession of three British battleships flanked by eight destroyers. Displaying consummate nerve, Tiesenhausen eased his boat at periscope depth between two destroyers and, from 1,200 yards, fired four torpedoes at the middle battleship in the line, the *Barham*. Three hit home.

As usual, the submarine's bow shot upward after the weight was released. Tiesenhausen could not get it down fast enough, and the conning tower erupted from the water barely 150 yards in front of the third battleship in line, the *Valiant*, whose captain immediately altered course in order to ram. The U-boat's engineers moved quickly to get their boat under again as the huge ship turned in a wide arc and bore down on them. Agonizing seconds passed. Then, at the last possible moment, the U-boat slid beneath the waves, and the battleship passed harmlessly overhead. Meanwhile, a fourth explosion, probably the magazine going up, disintegrated the *Barham*, killing 862 men.

Aboard the U-331, something odd was happening to the depth gauge. As the boat continued its crash dive, the needle indicating depth inexplicably slowed, then stopped at 250 feet. The crew sensed that the boat was still diving, but the gauge said not. It was a dangerous situation, because the boat's maximum safe depth was judged to be 330 feet. Tiesenhausen asked to have a second, forward depth gauge read. The report appalled the entire crew: They had reached the unprecedented depth of 820 feet. As they frantically halted the dive and began to ascend again, the hull, which should have been crushed at that depth, did not so much as spring a leak. The U-boat had escaped from the enemy above and the lethal pressure below. "In such moments, you do not speak," wrote Tiesenhausen many years later. "You are glad to have been lucky and to be still alive."

Despite these heady successes against Britain's finest warships, Dönitz continued to argue that his boats belonged not in the Mediterranean, but in the Atlantic. During November and December, he lost nine U-boats, one-third of the total now assigned to the Mediterranean. Meanwhile, fuel oil, ammunition, food, and other useful goods streamed virtually un-

A sequence of photographs taken from a British warship records the death throes of the battleship HMS *Barham,* sunk by Freiherr von Tiesenhausen's U-331 near the Egyptian coast in November 1941. Struck by three torpedoes, the *Barham* began to sink, and within five minutes its magazine blew the ship apart.

touched across the Atlantic. To the extent that he could without ending his career, Dönitz made clear his frustration.

"The most important task of the German navy," he wrote years later with undiminished fervor, "the task that overshadowed everything else, was the conduct of operations against shipping on Britain's vital lines of communication across the Atlantic. It was along them that flowed the sources of British strength, provided for the most part by American power." To remove the U-boats from the Atlantic, where they had been exacting a heavy toll, "was, in my opinion, completely unjustifiable."

Yet Dönitz's submarines were making their presence felt in the Mediterranean. Although Rommel had to retreat west of Tobruk in early December, German submarines were crippling British naval forces in those waters. Prime Minister Churchill gravely reported to the House of Commons that seven capital ships, one-third of the Mediterranean fleet, had been put out of action. Little more than a handful of cruisers and destroyers were still operating. German convoys were getting through to Rommel.

Thus both the German U-boat command and the British Admiralty were already mired in gloom when they received the electrifying news on December 7, 1941, of Japan's attack on Pearl Harbor. The surprise was as complete in the capital of the Reich, Berlin, as it was in Allied capitals, because Japan had given its Axis partner no warning of the move that would drastically change the course of the war.

Dönitz had been itching to strike at the "American power" that was bolstering Britain. As early as September of 1941, he had proposed sending his boats into waters close to the United States, but permission had been denied. He and Raeder protested Hitler's passivity in the face of the increasingly aggressive American support of British convoys, which by late 1941 had led to an undeclared state of war at sea. Still, Hitler forbade intentional attacks on American ships.

That changed after Pearl Harbor. On December 11, although it was not technically required by their alliance with Japan, Germany and Italy declared war on the United States. Dönitz was ready with plans for a U-boat operation he called *Paukenschlag*, or Drumbeat. He wanted to assign twelve of the big type-IX boats, which had a range of 8,000 to 13,000 miles, to American waters. Instead, the high command ordered even more U-boats to the Mediterranean, leaving only five of the big boats to operate in the western Atlantic.

Dönitz grimly prepared this small force for its unaided assault on Germany's newest and most formidable enemy. He handpicked the captains and briefed them himself. They were to take up stations between the mouth of the Saint Lawrence River in the north and Cape Hatteras in the south, then sink every ship they could find. On January 13, 1942, the first two submarines arrived off the eastern coast of the United States. The U-boat captains could scarcely believe their good fortune. After two years of

Outfitting the Gray Wolves

The harsh environment of a U-boat required special clothes and gear. Cold-weather duty in the North Atlantic called for warm, protective clothing, and the machine-filled interior required easily cleaned denims that could withstand dirt, oil, and grease. Each boat also carried special-issue gear, ranging from waterproof foul-weather coats and suits *(right)* to inflatable life jackets and emergency-escape devices *(center)*. Although the choice of clothing at sea was informal, the German admiralty tried to maintain some standards for its officers and ordered boat captains to wear at least portions of the uniform appropriate to their rank.

These wool-lined coat and trousers, made of treated leather, were issued to deck personnel. Most U-boat sailors favored the blue forage cap, adorned with homemade versions of their boat or flotilla's insignia.

war in Europe and more than a month after Pearl Harbor, the Americans were behaving as though the world were at peace. With scant protection, tankers and cargo ships steamed heedlessly up and down the coast, lights ablaze, officers chatting freely on their radios about their ships' positions, courses, and cargoes. Navigational beacons and markers remained complacently lit, as did the glowing signs and lights of the ports, villages, and seaside resorts from Maine to Miami.

At 1:30 a.m. on January 14, a U-boat on the surface sixty miles off Long Island's Montauk Point struck a killing blow with a single torpedo aimed at the unsuspecting Panamanian tanker *Norness.* A perfect hit holed the vessel, set it afire, and sent it quickly to the bottom. The *Norness* was the first of thirteen tankers and freighters to go down in the United States' coastal waters during the next seventeen days.

Germans called it the "Second Happy Time" and the "American Shooting Season." Day and night, U-boats prowled the coastline, listening to the informative chatter on the radio bands, then selecting worthwhile targets

The escape apparatus, which served as life jacket and re-breather, had an oxygen cylinder and a canister of carbon dioxide-absorbent chemicals. The wearer breathed through the mouthpiece at center.

Officers wore the reefer (*right*) as semiformal dress; many kept a worn one for use on board. Wartime regulations permitted only a blue cap cover, but the prewar white summer cover became the trademark of a U-boat skipper.

and opening fire. Wreckage, oil slicks, and bodies began drifting ashore along the East Coast, but the Americans seemed incapable of responding. It was inconceivable that the U-boats could strike this close to home. Although the British had amply warned of the pending danger based on decoded radio signals, nothing had been done.

The warships of the U.S. Navy's Atlantic Fleet had been committed to serve as escorts for transatlantic convoys or to confront the enemy's surface navy. They were not available for coastal defense. The 1,500-mile shoreline between the Canadian border and North Carolina was guarded by only 20 Coast Guard cutters and 103 antiquated airplanes. Orders to ships of the Merchant Marine to run without lights were ignored because it was inconvenient. Orders to civilians ashore to douse their lights at night were disregarded because blackouts would have been bad for the tourist business. The shooting season continued.

On the evening of February 4, the oil tanker *Indian Arrow* steamed northward off the Jersey shore. To port, the lights of Atlantic City glowed on the horizon like an artificial sunset. To starboard, the waters of the Atlantic rolled black and ominous. It could not have been a restful time for the crew; a few days before, a merchant ship had been sunk nearby when a U-boat surfaced 200 yards away and attacked with its deck gun until the merchantman went down. Hours earlier, in the same waters, a freighter had taken a torpedo and sunk.

At half past six, a U-boat watched the *Indian Arrow*, silhouetted starkly against the distant city's lights, move into its torpedo sights. The U-boat's forward tube disgorged at least one torpedo that found its mark. The exploding projectile put a hole in the tanker below the water line, and shells from the U-boat's deck gun set its leaking cargo afire. Within minutes, the ship was listing heavily and surrounded by ponds of burning oil. The crew launched two lifeboats and rowed for safety. Groaning like a wounded leviathan, the sinking tanker rolled onto one of the lifeboats, taking it and its crew down with it. The men in the other boat pulled hard for 300 feet before they passed beyond the rim of fire, then set course for the lights of Atlantic City, which were not as close as they looked. A day and a half later, a fishing boat picked up the survivors. In the meantime, another torpedoed tanker went to the bottom near the hulk of the *Indian Arrow*.

The extent of the offshore carnage and the Americans' inability to do anything about it were becoming widely known despite the efforts of military censors to suppress the bad news. In early February, the crews of six merchant ships in New York Harbor refused to sail until they were protected from the U-boats. The navy belatedly assigned seven destroyers to coastal defense. But the United States had nowhere near enough armed

Broken in half by a German torpedo, the American tanker *Dixie Arrow* goes down in flames off North Carolina on March 26, 1942. Submariners found the pickings so easy along the American coast they called this period the "Second Happy Time."

ships to protect the heavy traffic along the East Coast. For the most part, the Coastal Command had to be content with urging the merchant captains to turn off their running lights, stay off their radios, sail close to shore, and hope for the best. The anemic American response to the threat contrasted starkly to the British reaction. Churchill understood at once that Dönitz had found an Achilles heel and that, unless something were done, the U-boats in American waters could wreck the effort to ship supplies to Britain. Though hard-pressed on every front, the British found some underused, coal-burning fishing trawlers and dispatched them to the United States. With the addition of depth-charge catapults and asdic equipment, they would be converted for antisubmarine duty.

Hitler, meanwhile, dispersed Dönitz's forces once again. The Führer became convinced that the Allies were planning to invade Norway, which he said would be the "zone of destiny" in which the "issue of the war" would be settled. In January and February of 1942, he ordered a dozen U-boats sent to Norwegian waters and eight more to the area between Iceland and the Hebrides to await the Allied attack. Several of these boats had been destined for American waters. Even as Dönitz protested the disruption of his Operation Drumbeat, a fresh wave of his raiders arrived in the Caribbean. Their destination was the Trinidad-Aruba-Curaçao area, a prime source of oil shipments. Petroleum products that were stored, refined, or transshipped in the Caribbean moved from there to the east coast of the United States and then in guarded convoys to Britain.

Again, the appearance of the U-boats seemed to come as a shock. On February 16, German submarines sank six tankers off Maracaibo and two more ships near Port of Spain and shelled the oil refinery at Aruba. The carnage spread north to the coast of Florida, and in February 470,000 tons were lost in American waters, 30 percent more than in January. Other U-boats pounded plentiful targets from the Carolinas north. The coastal freighters and tankers kept coming to the slaughter, without escorts. A few vessels were fitted with guns, a move whose dubious wisdom was revealed on March 18, when a merchant ship mistook a U.S. Navy destroyer for a submarine and sent a shell into its bridge, killing the captain. Some antisubmarine patrols were organized, but they had little equipment and less experience. On February 28, action involving an aircraft, a Coast Guard cutter, and a navy destroyer resulted in the depth-charging of a whale.

Stripped to their skivvies in the tropical heat, crewmen on the U-461, a type-XIV tanker, monitor the refueling of a U-boat while a second one awaits its turn. The so-called milk cows could resupply a dozen medium-size boats, doubling their time at sea.

March brought additional bounty to the dozen or so U-boats operating off the East Coast and in the Caribbean. They sank as much shipping as in January and February combined—seventy-nine ships. An American study committee predicted the loss of 3,000 seafarers' lives by the end of the year, along with 125 of the 300 tankers serving the East Coast. In Britain, the prospect of running out of oil became very real. "I am most deeply concerned," Churchill pronounced, and he sent five corvettes to help the Americans defend themselves.

By April, the first of the converted fishing trawlers were ready for duty and became the nucleus of a limited convoy system. The escorts shepherded the merchant ships during the day and sheltered them in harbors at night. The system was poorly organized, but it reduced the number of easy opportunities for the waiting submarines. As the additional British sub-hunters arrived, the convoy lifeline was extended as far as Key West.

Slowly, the Americans sharpened their defenses, as the U-85 discovered on the night of April 13. Lieutenant Eberhard Greger had arrived off the coast a week earlier and sunk a merchantman on April 10, but he was finding the pickings slimmer than expected. Eager to seek out targets and contemptuous of American defenses, Greger sailed submerged near the entrance to Chesapeake Bay, not far from the home of the U.S. Navy's Atlantic Fleet. No sooner had he surfaced, off Nags Head, than he was attacked by an American destroyer.

The USS *Roper*, having picked up the U-boat on both sonar and radar, closed so unexpectedly that Greger did not have time to dive. He had to run on the surface, twisting and turning desperately to gain the room to submerge at a reasonable distance from the destroyer's depth charges. But the *Roper* stayed with his feverish zigzags, refusing to be thrown off, slowly closing the gap until the submarine was within range of the ship's guns. Machine-gun fire cut down the U-boat's deck gunners, and three-inch shells crashed into its hull and conning tower. The boat began to sink, and crew members clambered out of hatches and jumped into the water. When the U-85 slipped below the surface, it left behind an oil slick and forty men struggling in the water. To make sure of its kill, the *Roper* dropped eleven depth charges over the oil slick where the U-85 went down. None of the U-boat's crew survived.

Dönitz had lost his first submarine in American waters. Far from daunted, he and his captains pressed the hunt. In the first ten days of April, they had sent seven more tankers to the bottom. On April 22, their effectiveness was doubled by the arrival near Bermuda of a tanker-submarine carrying 700 tons of fuel oil. Now the U-boats did not have to trek to their French ports to refuel; they had only to meet the milk cow, as they dubbed the

An American patrol boat pursuing a submarine contact fires a depth charge from the Y-gun on its forward deck. During the first half of 1942, submarine-hunters in American waters sank an average of one U-boat a month.

U-tanker. As long as a boat had torpedoes and basic supplies, it could remain on station off the American coast.

Fewer targets were visible in the sea lanes now, however, especially on the northern stations. The convoy system was slowly taking hold. Air patrols were more frequent, warships more numerous. On April 29, the U.S. Navy prohibited unescorted tanker traffic north of the Straits of Florida. But for a time, hunting remained good in the south. When the U-333 surfaced off Miami on the night of May 4, Captain Peter Erich Cremer wrote that his crew members "rubbed their eyes in disbelief." In startling contrast to blacked-out Europe, the shoreline was ablaze with light. The buoys and lighthouses shone brightly, and the glow from the city lit up the sky. From their conning tower, the astonished submariners used their night glasses to count automobile headlights and read neon signs. "Against this footlight glare of a carefree new world," Cremer wrote, "were passing the silhouettes of ships recognizable in every detail and as sharp as the outlines in a sales catalog. Here they were formally presented to us on a plate: Please help yourselves! All we had to do was press the button."

Over the next three days, the U-333 sank three tankers. Two other U-boats nearby sent nine more ships to their graves. The sea was littered with wreckage and covered with oil slicks that sometimes caught fire, creating palls of smoke that darkened the sun. People lazing on the Florida beaches saw conning towers in broad daylight and excitedly called in reports that were useless because it took the authorities too long to respond. On May 6, civilians watched a U-boat sink two tankers off Jupiter Inlet, one of them going down so close to shore its masts were visible when its keel struck bottom. That day, the U.S. Navy forbade unescorted merchant vessels to sail in the Straits of Florida and the Gulf of Mexico.

Farther north, the U-boats waited in vain. The captain of the U-352 patrolled so long off Cape Hatteras without seeing a target that he attacked

Shaken by their ordeal, German crew members rest on the deck of a U.S. Coast Guard cutter after being rescued from the North Atlantic. The cutter had sunk their U-boat with depth charges.

the first vessel he spotted, on May 9. His prey turned out to be a Coast Guard cutter, the USS *Icarus*, which turned on the U-boat and quickly sank it. The rate of U-boat losses was in fact rising just as the number of sinkings declined. The equation that Dönitz watched most closely—the number of tons of enemy shipping sunk per day per submarine—was also shrinking. If hunting did not remain extraordinarily good in American waters, then the long transatlantic voyages of the boats, during which they sank nothing, reduced the entire fleet's performance.

In the first six months of 1942, German submarines had sunk 585 Allied ships, averaging 500,000 tons a month. More than half of these kills came in the western Atlantic and the Caribbean. In the process, the Germans had lost only six U-boats. It had been a magnificent shooting season, but by the middle of July, Dönitz knew it was over. He ordered his boats to withdraw from American coastal waters, mining the shipping lanes as they left to continue the destruction for a while.

For all his successes, Dönitz was a worried man in the summer of 1942. He still had not won his superiors' support for his basic premises—that victory depended upon destroying the enemy's merchant ships, and that the most effective weapon for the purpose was the U-boat. "The result of the war," he declared, "will depend on the result of the race between sinkings and new construction." He noted that even though the Allies were losing 500,000 tons of shipping a month, they were launching more ships than the Germans could destroy. According to German estimates, the United States, Britain, and Canada were building 700,000 tons of new shipping every month. The correct figure was 590,000 tons, but even at that, the Germans would have to sink even more to reduce the enemy's capacity.

Dönitz believed that the key was to concentrate the U-boats on the most vulnerable shipping lanes. When the Allies organized and defended one area, as they had done off the coast of the United States, he would attack another. Now, for example, the Allies had shifted so many escorts away from the North Atlantic convoy routes that those lanes were once again ripe for assault. But Dönitz never had enough boats. New ones had entered service at the satisfying rate of 20 a month during the last half of 1941. But a harsh winter hampered construction and training so·severely that for the first half of 1942 the pace slipped to 11.5 boats a month. And despite Dönitz's protests, 40 percent of the new boats were sidetracked either to Norway or to the Mediterranean.

Dönitz had also detected ominous improvements in the effectiveness of Allied submarine-hunting. His first clue came at the end of February, when the U-82, on its way home from Atlantic patrol, sighted a small convoy west

Senior British officers and their staff track the campaign in the Atlantic from the War Room of the Commander in Chief, Western Approaches, at Derby House in Liverpool. On the ladder, a member of the Women's Royal Naval Service updates the positions of Allied convoys and the estimated locations of wolf packs —based on intercepted radio traffic and other intelligence.

of the Bay of Biscay. The U-82 reported to headquarters that the convoy appeared to be only lightly protected. But after a short while, the U-boat's signals simply stopped. Something had destroyed it so quickly it had not had time to even send a distress call.

The incident might have been written off as one of the war's many small mysteries had it not been repeated, a month later, in the same area. This time, the U-587 reported that it was following a small convoy; then the submarine vanished. When a third boat, the U-252, sent a similar message on April 15, Dönitz warned the captain to be careful. That boat, too, was never heard from again. Dönitz interrogated returning crews and captains still at sea. But he could not account for these mystifying losses. He did not know that his missing U-boats had encountered Huff-Duff, the electronic detection device the British used to intercept radio transmissions. In practice, two stations picked up U-boat radio signals, and the cross bearings that resulted revealed the position of the submarine. Until 1942, the bearings were taken from shore stations at long distance and were not very accurate. But now the British were installing Huff-Duff sets on their escort ships. Intercepting signals at short range from a source making long and frequent transmissions, as U-boats did when shadowing a convoy, Huff-Duff proved to be deadly accurate.

Other troublesome attacks were occurring in the Bay of Biscay. For more than a year, the Royal Air Force had patrolled the bay, searching, among other things, for U-boats going to and from their French bases. But the pilots could not see the submarines at night, and in the daytime, lookouts could usually spot the aircraft in time for the boat to dive. In the spring of 1942, however, an increasing number of subs were surprised by planes coming out of nowhere, with guns firing, as if the pilot had honed in on the target from afar. Either all U-boat lookouts had suffered a sudden decline in alertness or the enemy had developed something new.

In June, all doubt was removed. The deck watch of a U-boat, cruising in the presumed safety of a dark night, heard a plane approaching. No precautions seemed necessary, and none were taken. Then, when the plane was about a thousand yards away, the comforting darkness was pierced by the beam of a searchlight mounted on the aircraft. Before the crew could react, their boat was bracketed by bombs and severely damaged. Two more U-boats soon had similar experiences. Dönitz recorded in his war diary that the Bay of Biscay had suddenly become the "happy hunting ground of the Royal Air Force."

A British airman cleans the lens of a Leigh light slung under the wing of a Coastal Command bomber. Named for its inventor, Humphrey de Verde Leigh, the powerful searchlight could illuminate a surfaced U-boat at night almost a mile away.

A high-frequency direction finder (HF/DF) clings like a spider web to a British destroyer's main mast. The electronic device, known as Huff-Duff, could tune in on radio transmissions between U-boats and their headquarters, enabling the British to get a fix on the boats' locations.

The British had developed a startling new capability for finding U-boats on the surface, even in bad weather and at night, at unprecedented range and with unheard-of accuracy. Dönitz correctly concluded that his foe had deployed an improved airborne radar that, in conjunction with the so-called Leigh light, was accounting for the German losses in the Bay of Biscay. The only defense his technical staff could quickly devise was a radar detector called Metox. Each U-boat was soon equipped with a receiver connected to a makeshift direction-finding antenna of wire wrapped around a wooden frame. This so-called Biscay Cross, when deployed on the conning tower of a surfaced submarine, picked up any incoming radar signals and sent them to the receiver, warning the crew to submerge before the enemy aircraft appeared.

By October, the new detectors had reduced the losses of submarines in the Bay of Biscay, but now the boats had to run submerged much of the time. Underwater, they were slow and clumsy, and their range was extremely limited. Only on the surface could they move fast enough and far enough to catch a convoy, escape a warship, or cross an ocean. And the Allies stepped up the pressure. In addition to their new detectors, they deployed planes with twice the range common early in the war and sent aircraft along with their convoys on new escort carriers. They were also using better munitions—more effective depth charges and new rockets. "These ever-increasing difficulties," Dönitz wrote in his war diary, "can only lead to intolerable losses, to a decrease in the volume of our success, and to a diminution, therefore, of our chances of victory in the U-boat war as a whole." On June 24, he sent a memorandum to his superiors raising the question of whether, as he put it, "the submarine, with its present power as an instrument of war, is equal to the heavy demands being made of it." He pointed out that the effectiveness of the new British radar (he did

not yet know about the increased use of Huff-Duff) meant the end of wolf-pack tactics, because a U-boat could no longer remain on the surface long enough to get in position to attack a convoy. He predicted that new merchant vessels would be even faster and more difficult to catch.

A remedy for these difficulties, Dönitz suggested, was a submarine that could move fast enough while submerged to catch and attack convoys. As Dönitz knew, such a submarine had been designed on paper before the war. Professor Helmuth Walter of Kiel had proposed replacing the cumbersome dual system of diesel engines for surface running and slower electric motors for underwater propulsion. His solution was a single, powerful engine that burned hydrogen peroxide, a liquid fuel that contained

A U.S. Navy blimp provides a vigilant eye in the evening sky above an Atlantic convoy. By 1942, a typical convoy was organized in a rectangular pattern (*right*), with escort ships spread around the perimeter. Ammunition ships, oil tankers, and troop transports were positioned inside the formation for relative safety. In rough weather, or when U-boats attacked, the precise spacing was almost impossible to maintain.

its own oxygen and thereby made an outside supply of air unnecessary. Walter believed his boat could make twenty-four knots underwater and do so for six hours at a time. But he had been unable to interest the naval high command in producing his design.

Dönitz concluded his memo with a plea: "The immediate development, testing, and most rapid construction of the Walter U-boat is, in my opinion, an essential measure and one that may decide the whole issue of the war." But the admiral knew that, even in the unlikely event his recommendation were approved, it would have no immediate effect. Resolving as always to do the best he could with what he had, Dönitz once more focused his attention on the North Atlantic. Convoys had resumed using the Great Circle route, the shortest distance between Newfoundland and Britain. Thus Dönitz knew exactly where enemy shipping was concentrated and most vulnerable—especially after German navy cryptographers had broken the British code and could intercept convoy communications. He also had more boats with which to attack. On July 1, 331 boats were in commission, 101 of them available for Atlantic duty—theoretically, an average of 19 on station, 40 en route to or from their stations, and 42 in port for repair and resupply. Moreover, German yards recovered at last from the setbacks of the winter and began to deliver 30 new boats a month.

Dönitz instructed his raiders to gather in packs at midocean, beyond the range of even the newest land-based aircraft. In this unprotected zone, the

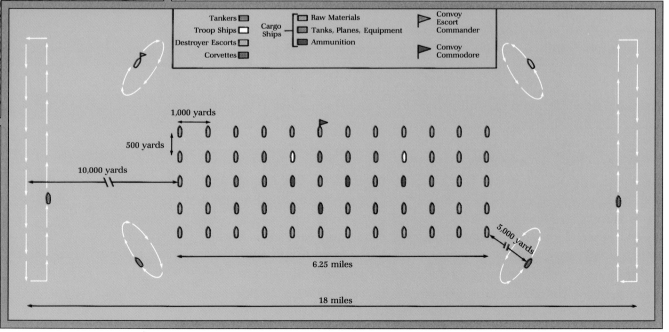

German submarines would make contact with the convoys and track them to the fringe of Allied air cover, sniping as they went. The return of U-boats to the North Atlantic was no surprise to the Allies. British analysts had begun to understand Dönitz's strategy and had predicted the new stage of the war at sea well in advance. But there was little they could do. The Allies lacked the extra fuel and escort ships required on the longer, more evasive routes that had helped them evade the wolf packs in 1941. The endless demand for supplies required six convoys a month of about fifty vessels each, protected at all times by at least seven armed escorts. The Allies were hard-pressed to keep the minimum number of escort destroyers and corvettes in service, much less provide additional protection. They would simply have to endure the worst the U-boats could give.

During July and August, Dönitz found that he could mount only one patrol at a time, with a pack of twelve to eighteen boats. But he added ten boats a month to his fleet, until in October he had forty at sea and as many as four wolf packs operating simultaneously. Despite this increasing coverage, a streak of bad weather in September made it virtually impossible for the boats to find or attack anything. And for a time, Dönitz was distracted by an event in the South Atlantic that would cast a long shadow over him and his seamen.

The admiral had stationed a contingent of U-boats along the west coast of Africa, where the northbound cargo ships coming around the Cape of Good Hope converged off Freetown, Sierra Leone. On the morning of September 12, the U-156, commanded by Werner Hartenstein, was cruising southward on the surface off the African coast when a lookout reported smoke on the southwest horizon. The ship he sighted was bearing northwestward and was 500 miles from the coast, outside the normal shipping lanes and the area that was usually patrolled by Allied planes based at Freetown. Hartenstein brought his boat to a parallel course and kept the smoke in sight, staying far behind the distant ship until he could close with it after night had fallen.

Hartenstein would soon discover that his prey was the *Laconia*, a Cunard passenger liner of 20,000 tons that at the outbreak of war had been armed with eight guns, depth charges, and asdic equipment and fitted out as a troop transport. The *Laconia* was making its way from Suez to England, heavily laden with nearly 3,000 souls on board. Among them were 286 British servicemen returning home; 80 civilians, including women and children; and, jammed in the hold, 1,800 Italian prisoners of war bound for internment. As the ship steamed through calm seas under a tropical sun, everyone on board was aware of the threat of U-boat attack. But in the month they had been at sea, apprehension had given way to boredom and

Lieut. Commander Werner Hartenstein, shown on the bridge of his U-156, initiated one of the sea war's most controversial episodes on September 12, 1942, when he sank the converted liner *Laconia*, on its way to England from British Africa. Hartenstein tried to rescue the survivors, who included British civilians, Italian prisoners, and Polish guards. But an American B-24 ignored flashing signals, radio messages, and a Red Cross flag and bombed the sub, damaging it and blowing up a lifeboat. In retaliation, Dönitz ordered his boats not to assist their victims.

routine. No one suspected the presence of the sharklike profile just below the glittering horizon.

Hartenstein neared his target as sunset approached. With no escort ships or aircraft to worry about, the German commander enjoyed the prospect of a riskless attack. It was simply a matter of sighting on the target with the on-deck telescope, setting the torpedoes for course, then firing tubes one and three. At a range of about two miles, it would take the torpedoes three minutes to make their run. Once they were away, Hartenstein pushed his cap back on his head and said, "Enjoy your meal, my dear Englishmen."

Crew members of the U-156 saw a geyser of foaming water leap up alongside the *Laconia* and fall away to reveal a gaping, jagged hole amidships. Then the second torpedo hit, with somewhat less spectacular effect. The *Laconia* stopped dead in the water and began to list. Hartenstein congratulated himself and ordered his submarine forward in order to complete its mission; he must identify the stricken ship and try to capture its captain and chief engineer.

The U-boat was still a mile from the sinking liner when it entered a hellish scene. The sea was littered with pieces of wreckage, floating corpses, overloaded lifeboats, and frantic swimmers. Calls for help and screams of panic rent the night—sharks and five-foot-long barracuda were slashing at the swimmers. Appalled, Hartenstein resolved to remain only long enough to see the ship go down, confirming his kill; then he would leave the area. Surely, the liner had reported its distress, and aircraft might be on the way to attack him. Then the captain heard, among the shouts from the water, cries for help in Italian: "Aiuto, aiuto!" Puzzled, he ordered a few survivors taken aboard and learned of the presence of the prisoners of war. He saw women and children aboard boats and rafts in the water. At that point, he decided to honor a tradition of the sea older than the war; despite the danger of attack, he began taking on survivors.

When Hartenstein's radio report of his rescue effort reached Dönitz's operations center in Paris, it triggered an unprecedented conflict between the U-boat chief and his staff. Although Dönitz had ordered U-boats not to endanger themselves by attempting rescues, this time he relented. "Once Hartenstein had begun the rescue operation," Dönitz explained years later, "I couldn't have ordered him to break it off. The morale of my men was very high, and to give them an order contrary to the laws of humanity would

have destroyed it utterly. My general staff did not agree with me. I remember one officer thumping the table, red with fury." Dönitz not only permitted the U-156 to continue the rescue—it already had ninety survivors aboard—but ordered three more U-boats to speed to Hartenstein's aid. It would take three days for the nearest of them to arrive.

During that time, Hartenstein maneuvered the U-156 among the scattered lifeboats and rafts. The German captain reassured the shipwrecked that rescue was imminent, provided them with water and food, and took on the wounded and most desperate until 263 survivors were aboard his

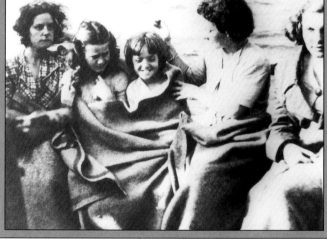

Survivors line the deck of the U-506 (top), one of several vessels that came to the rescue of the *Laconia* off Africa's west coast. Women and children wrapped in blankets (above) were among those saved by German boats.

cramped boat. He broadcast a promise not to attack any ship helping in the rescue, so long as he was not attacked. Startled by this tactic, Dönitz nevertheless supported it, stipulating only that neither Hartenstein nor any other German commander take on so many people that he could not dive if necessary. Dönitz's position was made more difficult when he received curt orders, relayed from Adolf Hitler, not to risk a U-boat during the rescue operation. On September 15, a second boat, the U-506, arrived and began to assist in the rescue.

At midday on September 16, a four-engine Liberator bomber with American markings flew low over the U-156 and the four crowded lifeboats it had under tow. Hartenstein had draped a huge flag displaying a Red Cross over the forward gun, and he signaled the B-24, appealing for help with the rescue. The plane flew away without answering. Half an hour later, it, or another like it, appeared and headed for the U-boat. Hartenstein expected a drop of food and medicine or at least news of assistance. Instead, he saw the bomb-bay doors open and bombs arcing toward him. Two missed, but the Liberator made a second pass. This time, it scored a direct hit on one of the lifeboats. Another of its bombs burst directly beneath the submarine. The U-156 was damaged, taking on water, and helplessly exposed to further attack. Hartenstein ordered all survivors off his boat. When they were clinging to the remaining lifeboats or adrift in the water, he made what repairs he could, submerged, and departed.

Two other U-boats, the U-506 and U-507, remained in the area. They were laden with survivors, towing lifeboats, and unwilling to desert the people they had saved. The Vichy French government had promised to dispatch rescue ships from Dakar, but the U-boat commanders were uncertain when the French vessels would arrive. Meanwhile, they had orders from Dönitz not to risk their boats. Not until September 17, five harrowing days after the sinking of the *Laconia*, did French ships arrive and take on survivors—thus freeing the German boats. Of the 2,732 passengers aboard the *Laconia* when it went down, 1,111 were saved—although two of its lifeboats, carrying twenty souls, were not found for a month. Dönitz realized that he must never again let his U-boats be caught in such a compromising situation. In the future, he ordered, "no attempt of any kind must be made to rescue the crews of ships sunk. Rescue runs counter to the primary demands of warfare for the destruction of enemy ships and their crews." The admiral concluded the directive with the imprecation, "Be harsh, bearing in mind that the enemy takes no regard for women and children in his bombing attacks on German cities."

The Allies regarded Dönitz's order as a directive to kill survivors of torpedoed ships even if they were civilians. This interpretation seemed to be confirmed in the spring of 1944, when the U-852 sank the steamer *Peleus* and fired on the wreckage, heedless of the survivors in the water. Dönitz said later that the commander tried to sink the wreckage because it revealed his presence to air patrols. But when the boat's commander fell into British hands later that year, he was condemned for his action; after the war, he was shot. Dönitz, too, stood trial for the *Laconia* order, before the Nuremberg war-crimes tribunal. But he was found innocent of the charge that he had ordered the survivors to be murdered.

In the aftermath of the *Laconia* affair, Dönitz returned his attention to the North Atlantic, where the wolf packs roamed, and killed, beyond the range of land-based aircraft. To be sure, the U-boats failed to spot some convoys and did not organize successful attacks on others. But once a pack closed in, it was capable of causing incredible destruction. The cruise of Group Violet in the autumn of 1942 illustrated the point. The pack's fifteen boats waited off Newfoundland in late October, hoping to pick up an eastbound convoy. Hope became certainty when U-boat command received a decoded Allied message that revealed the makeup, route, and departure time from New York of convoy SC107. By October 30, the boats of Group Violet were positioned perfectly to intercept the forty-two-ship convoy, steaming in seven columns under the uncertain protection of an inexperienced and understrength Royal Canadian Navy escort—one destroyer and four corvettes. The U-522, commanded by Herbert Schneider, reached the convoy first and fell in behind it to guide the other members of the pack, issuing regular position reports and a homing signal.

Huff-Duff receivers both ashore and on board the *Restigouche*, the escort destroyer, picked up and plotted the first transmissions from the U-522. The convoy still sailed under the protective umbrella of Allied aircraft based in Newfoundland, and would for another forty-eight hours. Although bad weather interfered with air operations on October 31, a few planes got through to counter the gathering of the pack. The U-522 had to dive in order to escape one plane, thus risking loss of contact with the convoy, and two U-boats hurrying toward the rendezvous were caught on the surface and sunk in attacks from the air.

By evening on November 1, eight U-boats had gathered on the convoy's heels as the ships reached the edge of what seamen called the Black Pit or the Devil's Gorge—the 700-mile stretch of the North Atlantic that was beyond the reach of Allied aircraft. The men of the convoy knew that their defenses were now woefully inadequate. The perimeter of the convoy stretched for twenty-five miles; each of the five escorts had to cover five miles of water. But the range of their asdic gear was only about a quarter of that distance, and their radar range for surface detection was not much better. Additional escorts would have been helpful, but they had been sent elsewhere to take part in Operation Torch, the Allied invasion of North Africa, which was to occur in only a few days.

Hidden by darkness, all eight U-boats moved into attack position abreast of the convoy, and the crews of the merchantmen and escorts braced for the inevitable. Their ordeal began shortly after midnight. The U-402, commanded by Baron Siegfried von Forstner, crept past the corvette on station two miles from the convoy's starboard flank—a move made simple because the corvette's radar was not working. Forstner advanced to within 400 yards of a column of freighters, then fired. His first torpedo refused to leave the tube, a second ran erratically, but the third sped true to strike the freighter *Empire Sunrise* amidships. The resulting explosion showered the U-boat with debris and sent the freighter to its grave.

As flares called snowflakes arched into the sky from the convoy's ships and briefly illuminated the black waters below, nervous gunnery crews on the destroyer searched for a target. They saw nothing but soon felt the concussions of two more torpedoes hitting home. They watched a nearby ship burst into flame and the one behind it veer out of its column, its red breakdown lights glowing ominously.

The U-boats circled and probed. The cautious ones stood off and fired fans of torpedoes at the convoy, trusting that one or more of them would hit. The aggressive captains—Forstner in the U-402 and Schneider in the U-522—crept inside the escort screen, fired at point-blank range, and dived to avoid the scurrying escorts. The U-402 had already sunk three ships. Schneider put two torpedoes into a freighter. Forstner hit two more ships, then Schneider two more. One victim was a munitions carrier whose cargo exploded so forcefully that five captains in the convoy reported their ships torpedoed, and one ordered his crew to abandon ship before discovering that his vessel was untouched.

The nightmare ended at dawn. In daylight, the U-boats had to stay out of sight, yet remain on the surface to keep up with the convoy. When night fell, they would renew the hunt. Schneider, in the U-522, was the exception. Disdaining orthodox tactics, he ranged ahead of the convoy on the surface, then made a daylight submerged attack that sent a ninth ship down. The convoy's designated rescue ship, having picked up 250 seamen before dawn, searched the convoy's wake all day for more survivors.

During the day, the stricken convoy twisted and dodged through rain and fog, hoping against hope to shake off the savage pursuers. Indeed, soon after dark in thickening fog, a sudden fifty-degree turn accomplished just that. But one of the corvettes failed to execute the turn properly and sailed headlong into the massed convoy, its lights off and its radar inoperative. When the captain realized where he was, he turned on his running lights and fired a flare. The startled merchantmen around him responded with a barrage of snowflakes, then turned on their lights, too. The corvette managed to exit the other side of the convoy without being run down, but the U-boats spotted the fireworks and closed in again.

The convoy tried another evasive turn, but not all of its captains got the word, and the ships blundered out of formation, straggling blindly through the fog and the dark. Like hunters among a herd of stampeding elephants, the U-boats were suddenly endangered by their prey. Unable to find targets without risking collision, the U-boats sank no ships that night. Dawn, however, found the U-521 methodically slamming one torpedo after another into the remarkably resilient oil tanker *Hahira*. After a third hit, the ship finally sank. During the daylight hours of November 3, as the exhausted combatants prepared for another night of conflict, both sides received word that help was on the way. Dönitz had seen a chance to annihilate the convoy and dispatched another wolf pack of fifteen boats

that had been patrolling 500 miles to the east. Meanwhile, the convoy had gained two additional escorts—a late-arriving corvette and a destroyer detached from another convoy. A U.S. Coast Guard cutter and two destroyers also were en route from Iceland.

Night fell before the distant reinforcements could arrive. Not long after dark, Dietrich Lohmann took his U-89 on the surface into the heart of the convoy and let go five torpedoes. Only two hit, but one of them crippled the convoy commodore's ship, the ammunition-laden *Jeypore*. A second damaged but did not sink another freighter. Just before midnight, the U-132 made its first and last attack of the battle. Approaching the convoy's starboard flank, the U-boat released a fan of five torpedoes. All struck home. In rapid succession, three stricken ships, two of them hit twice, dropped out of line, burning and sinking. Half an hour later, one of them exploded with such terrific force that ships up to six miles away reported being torpedoed, and U-boats 200 feet underwater were jolted. Strangely, the U-132, which had caused such havoc, was never heard from again.

The wind and the seas rose during the early morning hours, favoring the convoy. Although the wolf pack mounted three more attacks, no torpedoes hit. By morning, the weather was so bad that the U-boats lost touch with the convoy and failed to find it again that day. At nightfall, the U-89 made contact, attacked, and sank another ship—the fifteenth to go down in the one-sided battle. It was the last. The rest of the pack did not renew contact until nearly dawn, and by then both the Allied warships and a Liberator bomber had arrived from Iceland. The aircraft attacked and damaged the U-89. Group Violet broke off the engagement and Dönitz diverted the second wolf pack to attack another convoy farther east. The twenty-seven ships remaining in convoy SC107—victim of the worst mauling by U-boats of any convoy in 1942—continued unmolested to their destination.

Dönitz, for a change, was well satisfied. He had just destroyed 81,000 tons of shipping in a single convoy at a cost of three U-boats. Year-end statistics would show that his wolf packs in all oceans had destroyed 1,160 Allied ships while losing 87 submarines. The Allies had lost 7.8 million tons of shipping and built about 7 million new tons. The fleet of operational U-boats had more than doubled in size, from 91 to 212. But any pleasure that Dönitz could take from his successes in the month of November was short-lived. German naval intelligence had failed to detect the Allies' preparations for a secret, massive strike, Operation Torch. Ironically, the blow fell in the area Dönitz had been struggling for more than a year to avoid— Gibraltar, the Mousetrap. On November 8, 1942, the largest amphibious landing to date was mounted in North Africa. And Dönitz had too few U-boats in the area to make a difference. ✠

Saga in the South Atlantic

One of the submarine war's most dramatic episodes was photographed by the German sailors and American airmen who participated in it. Their pictures of the saga are presented here and on the following pages.

In the summer of 1943, Admiral Karl Dönitz dispatched part of his U-boat fleet to the South Atlantic to hunt fresh prey in what were thought to be relatively safe conditions. But the waters off South America were full of unexpected perils; soon three of the German U-boats were themselves being hunted down. The action began on July 30, when a U.S. Navy bomber flying out of São Salvador, on the coast of Brazil, surprised the U-604 on the surface and dived to attack. The American plane raked the U-604 with machine-gun fire, killing two crewmen and wounding the captain, Horst Höltring. Then it bracketed the German boat with four Mark-47 depth bombs. His vessel crippled, Höltring radioed an emergency call for help: "Attacked by aircraft. Damaged. Ability to dive limited."

Two other submarines, the U-172 and U-185, responded to the appeal. Hounded by American destroyers and Brazil-based bombers, the would-be rescuers slipped and dodged through the southern seas for a week before the U-185, commanded by August Maus, surfaced near the U-604, took aboard its crew, and scuttled the doomed boat. After a few more days had passed, Maus rendezvoused with the U-172, whose navigational gear had been damaged. The two U-boats divided the survivors from the U-604 and began the 5,000-mile voyage to their bases on the coast of France.

The trials of Captain Maus and the U-185 had only begun. On August 24, short-range American fighters and bombers attacked the boat. They had taken off from a new weapon in the war at sea, an auxiliary carrier. Because his craft was severely damaged and sinking, Maus had to abandon ship and await rescue. Only the U-172 limped home to the sheltering pens at Lorient. With angry foreboding, one of Maus's fellow commanders blamed the loss of the two submarines on a "plague of enemy aircraft" that had "smashed our basic concept of U-boat warfare."

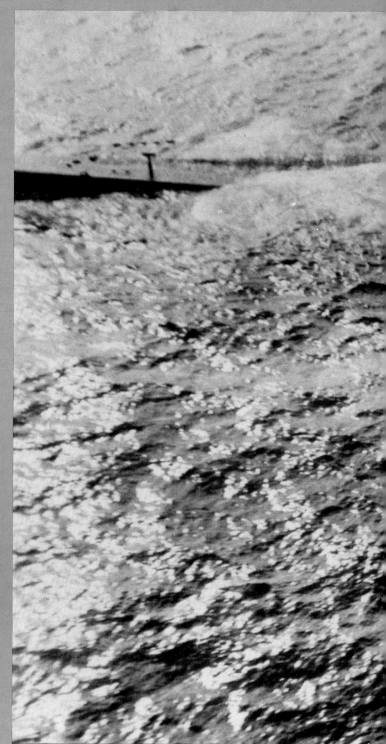

Half-submerged, the U-604 wallows in the South Atlantic after attacks

by a land-based PV-1 Ventura bomber like the one at top. The bombing wrecked one of the U-boat's engines and jammed its rudder.

His vessel overloaded after taking fuel, food, and the surviving crew off the U-604 before scuttling it, Captain Maus of the U-185 arranged by radio to meet with a third submarine, the U-172. A few days later, the two boats surfaced, standing some distance apart to ensure against collision and to have room to dive in case of enemy attack. Maus then ordered half of the U-604's men to swim to the other boat, an extraordinary transfer that a crew member of the U-172 photographed.

Heads bobbing above the surface (upper left), sailors from the U-604 swim from the U-185 (background) toward the U-172, some of whose crew members wait on deck to receive the swimmers.

Throwing out lifelines, crewmen on the U-172 help their fellow submariners, weary from swimming in waterlogged clothes, paddle the final yards to safety.

Some of the swimmers cling to life preservers as U-172 crew members strain to haul them up the sub's slippery hull.

The Sudden Demise of the U-185

The air attack on the surface-running U-185 came with breathtaking speed. A distant speck in the morning sky grew into a Grumman F4F Wildcat that roared down to pelt the submarine's exposed conning tower with .50-caliber bullets. All seven members of the bridge watch were killed or wounded before they could fire their guns or order a crash dive. Behind the Wildcat came a Grumman TBF Avenger, which dropped a depth bomb that ripped a hole in the U-boat's hull.

The fight was as good as over, but as additional planes from the auxiliary carrier *Core* circled and took photographs, the Wildcat strafed the stricken boat again, and the Avenger battered its hull with another depth bomb.

Inside, the U-185 was a nightmare. Chlorine gas, generated by water-soaked batteries, spread through the boat, killing some men immediately and poisoning others, who died later. Among those trapped was the wounded Captain Höltring of the U-604. As an act of mercy, he shot an injured sailor who could not flee the chlorine. Then Höltring turned his pistol and fired a bullet into his own head.

As men, gasping for air, scrambled up through the deck hatches of the sinking submarine, Maus ordered them over the side. An American destroyer picked thirty-six men from the sea; nine were originally survivors of the U-604.

Caught on the surface as it attempted to make a fast run home, the German U-185 lies

helpless in the Atlantic Ocean southwest of the Azores, its bow high and afterdeck awash in the roiling sea.

FOUR

The Last, Furious Gasp

arly in January 1943, storms of hurricane strength lashed the North Atlantic, halting the U-boat campaign against Allied convoys. In Berlin, Adolf Hitler erupted with comparable fury. Although the targets of his wrath were not the storm-buffeted submarines, but two of the sturdiest ships in the German navy, the results would profoundly affect the U-boat service. The Führer was incensed because on the last day of 1942, the pocket battleship *Lützow* and the heavy cruiser *Hipper* had allowed a convoy to escape virtually unscathed from an encounter in waters off Norway. Their failure was partly due to Hitler's instructions to proceed cautiously when faced with British opposition, but the Führer was not about to second-guess himself. He took out his anger on Erich Raeder, the navy's sixty-six-year-old grand admiral. He ordered Raeder to scrap all of Germany's remaining capital ships and turn their heavy guns into shore batteries. Raeder protested, and when Hitler refused to change his mind, the admiral resigned.

Hitler promptly chose Karl Dönitz as Raeder's successor, a move that provided the U-boats and their forceful leader with unprecedented opportunity. At age fifty-one, Dönitz was now in a position to focus the lion's share of the navy's resources on his wolf packs. It was his fierce conviction that only by building more and more U-boats could Germany turn the tide of war that was flowing against the Reich. Dönitz retained command of the submarines, and, in order to obtain the men and matériel to bolster them, he set out to win the Führer's trust. He did not find this task distasteful, because he was attracted to Hitler's "high intelligence and great energy." Unlike his reserved predecessor, who preferred to communicate through memorandums, Dönitz visited the Führer's headquarters frequently and eventually joined his inner circle. In their talks, Dönitz "found that it was a good idea to present my proposals in bold lines on a broad canvas, in a way that would excite Hitler's vivid powers of imagination."

The Führer liked his new top naval officer's optimism and toughness. At one of Dönitz's first conferences, Hermann Göring made a cutting remark about the navy. Unlike others who surrounded the Führer, Dönitz did not

An American coastguardsman helps a German sailor from the water minutes after his submarine went down in July 1943. The German still wears the breathing apparatus used to escape from a foundering U-boat.

Carrying the ornate baton (*above*) symbolizing his new rank as grand admiral of the German navy, Karl Dönitz continues his custom of greeting U-boat crews returning from patrol. After his 1943 promotion, Dönitz retained command of the U-boat force.

mince words. He barked back, telling the Luftwaffe chief to mind his own business. Only Hitler's chuckle broke the ensuing silence. What evidently sealed their relationship was Dönitz's iron will. Although he never questioned Hitler's overall strategy, he stuck to his guns in matters of importance to the navy, even on the issue that had forced Raeder's departure—the future of the capital ships. Deciding that it would be foolish to decommission them and thus free Allied planes and ships to fight the submarines, Dönitz persuaded Hitler to rescind his order. After that, Hitler, who meddled constantly with the army, rarely interfered in naval matters.

The most important concessions Dönitz won related to U-boat construction. The Führer increased the navy's allocation of steel and exempted from military service the skilled workers needed to build submarines. The key policy victory was Hitler's approval of a plan to transfer responsibility for the construction program from the navy itself to Albert Speer, minister for armaments and munitions. The decision was vindicated when Speer's builders began turning out nearly thirty U-boats a month, pushing the number of available boats to the level Dönitz had cited in 1939 as necessary to seriously challenge Allied shipping.

Dönitz would need every one of them. The Allies, meeting at Casablanca in January 1943, had accorded top priority to defeating the U-boats. Their most visible effort to implement this policy—bombing the bases on the Bay of Biscay—had little effect. The bombs could not penetrate the twenty-two-foot-thick concrete bunkers that housed the submarines, and no boats were destroyed. But the Allied antisubmarine forces had other measures in store as the struggle for the Atlantic shipping lanes grew in intensity.

While the appointment of Dönitz soothed Hitler and improved prospects for the U-boats, the weather over the North Atlantic also settled down. Because navigating small craft in the stormy seas had been so difficult, the U-boats sank only thirty-nine ships in January, and their score of 203,128 tons was the smallest monthly total in more than a year. By February, however, Dönitz had most of his boats back from the waters off Morocco's Atlantic ports and the approaches to the Strait of Gibraltar, where they had failed to slow the Allied invasion of North Africa the previous November. Of nearly 400 boats, more than 200 were operational, and 164 of those were assigned to the Atlantic. The greater numbers, sailing on calmer seas, paid off at once. In February of 1943, sixty-three ships of 359,328 tons went down.

It was not just the cold numbers but the exploits of a single boat, the U-402, that boosted morale in the U-boat command. The U-402 belonged to a pack of sixteen boats that on February 4 confronted a sixty-three-ship convoy bound from North America to the Soviet Union. An escort of eight

Raucous Rites at the Equator

In rough-and-tumble rites that provided a respite from war, U-boats heading into the South Atlantic observed nautical tradition by baptizing crewmen who were crossing the equator for the first time.

For the typical ceremony shown here, old hands dressed as Neptune, king of the sea, and Thetis, his mop-wigged queen, held court on the deck of the U-177. Their savage-looking helpers, wearing grass skirts, forced the neophytes to swallow large, foul-tasting pills and wash them down with cocktails of milk, salt water, and fuel oil. Then the initiates were shaved and drenched head to foot to cleanse them of the dirt of the Northern Hemisphere before they were welcomed into the Southern.

Even at this light moment, a submarine dared not drop its guard. Only half of the crew took part in the ceremony; the rest stayed below in order to keep the boat moving and ready to dive.

Admiral Triton greets the U-177's captain.

Senior seamen trim and spray an initiate.

King Neptune's motley court assembles on deck.

Queen Thetis smiles upon her bearded king.

A certificate of crossing.

147

British, Free French, and American warships—an unusually high number at this stage of the war—accompanied the convoy, designated SC118. The resulting clash was so furious that Dönitz would call it "perhaps the hardest convoy battle of the entire war."

For nearly three days, the Allied escorts had the better of the fight. The destroyers and other antisubmarine craft fended off the wolf pack, which had grown to a score of U-boats, sinking one attacker and damaging several others. Then, during the night of February 7, the U-402 went to work. Its commander was Baron Siegfried von Forstner, a Prussian aristocrat whose brother, Wolfgang, also commanded a U-boat. Forstner, who had sunk five Allied ships in November, was making his sixth war patrol. A former apprentice to the ace Otto Kretschmer, he was skilled at sneaking past the escorts and attacking from inside the convoy.

After midnight, Forstner found the starboard side of the convoy unprotected and maneuvered to within a mile of the closest ship. He began firing shortly after 2:00 a.m., his first torpedo claiming a small freighter. Two torpedoes missed a large tanker, but the next two hit and the tanker exploded. Penetrating a gap astern of the convoy, Forstner continued the hunt. Before dawn, the U-402 sank four more ships. With the sunrise came British air cover, and Forstner pulled back from the convoy. Later in the day, Dönitz radioed congratulations and the admonition "Stay tough."

Forstner did. Despite mechanical problems, the U-402 clung tenaciously to the convoy, somehow eluding the RAF Liberators that droned overhead for much of the day. That night, the U-boat caught up with a British merchantman and used its last torpedo to sink it. The following morning, February 9, the U-402, with its compressors leaking and one engine running on only five of its six cylinders, headed back to its base at La Pallice. Forstner had destroyed seven ships in less than twenty-four hours and increased the amount of shipping he had sunk to more than 100,000 tons. En route home, the commander received a radio message from Dönitz, who awarded him the Knight's Cross.

The heroics of February were prelude. The battle against convoy SC118 had cost Dönitz three boats lost and four heavily damaged. Thanks to Speer's construction program, he could replace the boats readily enough. But finding competent people to run them was another matter. By 1943, the war had stretched German manpower to the limit, and training time had to be reduced to keep pace with the rapid expansion of the fleet. More submarines were available, but they went to sea with inexperienced commanding officers and crews. Nonetheless, on March 1, 1943, Dönitz could count 70 U-boats on station worldwide and 114 in transit or in harbor. No fewer than 45 boats prowled the northern sea lanes, which were literally crowded with convoys. Every week, on average, two set sail eastbound and two returned. The U-boat scores mounted: During the first ten days of March, Dönitz's crews destroyed forty-one Allied ships. The struggle for the Atlantic was building to a crescendo.

The climactic battle—the largest of the war—would rage for five March days and pit 42 U-boats against more than 100 merchantmen and escorts. The interception of British radio traffic by B-Dienst, the German navy's cryptographic section, set the stage. The crucial messages—among the 175 Allied radio signals deciphered by B-Dienst during a three-week period—indicated that two eastbound convoys, SC122 and HX229, had left New York three days apart. They were heavy with vital war matériel: foodstuffs, locomotives, airplanes, and tanks.

Determined to bag both convoys, Dönitz on March 12 ordered deployment of the largest concentration of submarines ever, three wolf packs comprising thirty-eight U-boats. The first group, called *Raubgraf*, or Robber Baron, was to patrol northeastward off the Newfoundland coast. Farther east, the other two—*Stürmer*, or Daredevil, and *Dränger*, or Harrier—were to form picket lines in the mid-Atlantic gap, still 200 to 300 miles wide, that lay beyond the reach of land-based Allied aircraft. The two patrol lines would stretch 600 miles from north to south.

Baron Siegfried von Forstner, the fourth generation of an aristocratic Prussian family to enter the military, wears the white cap cover of a U-boat commander. Surprised by carrier-based American planes on October 13, 1943, Forstner crash-dived in his U-402, but one of the planes dropped a new acoustic torpedo that homed in on the boat's propeller noise and blew the submarine up with all aboard.

Dönitz did not reckon on the existence of a third convoy, which had split from HX229 before leaving New York and was the last to depart. Designated HX229A, it took the northernmost route and swung safely around the prowling submarines. The lead convoy, SC122, skirted the southern end of Raubgraf, the westernmost of the patrols. At first, its faster counterpart, HX229, also managed to elude Raubgraf's southern sentinels. On the stormy night of March 15, one of its portside destroyer escorts was sighted by the U-91, which gave chase with three other members of the pack. The Germans lost their quarry, however, and the convoy slipped by the Raubgraf line.

During the night, the two convoys—about 150 miles apart—sailed into the air gap between the German patrol lines, still undetected. Waiting to the east, the groups Stürmer and Dränger would almost certainly spot the convoys, but time was essential. Every hour brought the convoys nearer the eastern edge of the air gap, where they would come under the protection of Allied aircraft once more.

The lucky break the U-boats needed came in predawn darkness on March 16. One of the Raubgraf boats, the U-653, was steaming homeward on the surface. Low on gas, it had only one torpedo remaining and a defective diesel engine. Quartermaster Heinz Theen, commanding the bridge watch, made a startling discovery. "I saw a light directly ahead, for only about two seconds," he said later. "I think it was a sailor on the deck of a steamer lighting a cigarette. I sent a message to the captain, and by the time he had come up on the bridge, we could see ships all around us."

The U-653 had glided into the middle of the fast convoy, HX229, with its thirty-seven merchant ships escorted by three destroyers and two corvettes. The Germans scrambled below, went into an alarm dive, and then listened nervously as the ships of the convoy passed overhead. "We could hear quite clearly the noises of the different engines," recalled Theen, "the diesels with fast revs, the steamers with slow revs, and the turbines of the escorts making singing noises." The submarine waited for two hours until the convoy had passed. Then the boat surfaced to send off a short message in code that signaled a sighting and began to shadow HX229 on its northeast course at a speed of nine knots.

The radio alert emanated swiftly from Dönitz's new headquarters in Berlin's Hotel Am Steinplatz. Every boat in Raubgraf, Stürmer, and Dränger was ordered to converge on the convoy at maximum speed, and by dusk, the first seven hunters hovered near HX229. The moon rose nearly full to silhouette their targets. The two escorts guarding the starboard flank were six miles apart, and the U-603, under Lieut. Commander Hans-Joachim Bertelsmann, moved easily through the gap. Bertelsmann had already sunk two Norwegian tankers on his seven-week patrol and had only four torpedoes left. Three of them were FATs, short for *Federapparat*, or coiled-spring, torpedoes, which could be preset to steer in a straight line for a certain distance, then weave back and forth in a series of shallow loops. The torpedo was to cut back and forth across the path of a convoy until either it hit a ship or the power in its electric motor petered out. Before firing, a boat's radio operator routinely warned other U-boats in the vicinity so they could submerge and stand clear lest the torpedo zigzag into a friendly hull.

Inside the conning tower of the U-603, the watch officer, Rudolf Baltz, peered through the sighting glass. At 8:00 p.m., at the captain's command, Baltz fired the FATs in salvo. Just at that moment, however, the convoy was completing a turn, and all three of the missiles swerved away harmlessly. Seconds later, Baltz fired again, and the U-603's last torpedo, a conventional model, whooshed out of its tube, streaked straight ahead, and scored a direct hit. Within four minutes, the stricken freighter *Elin K.*, carrying 7,500 tons of wheat and manganese, stood on end and then corkscrewed down-

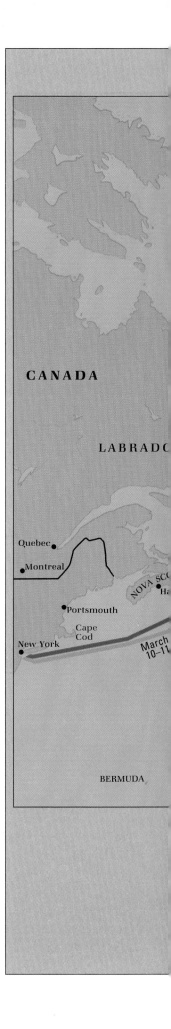

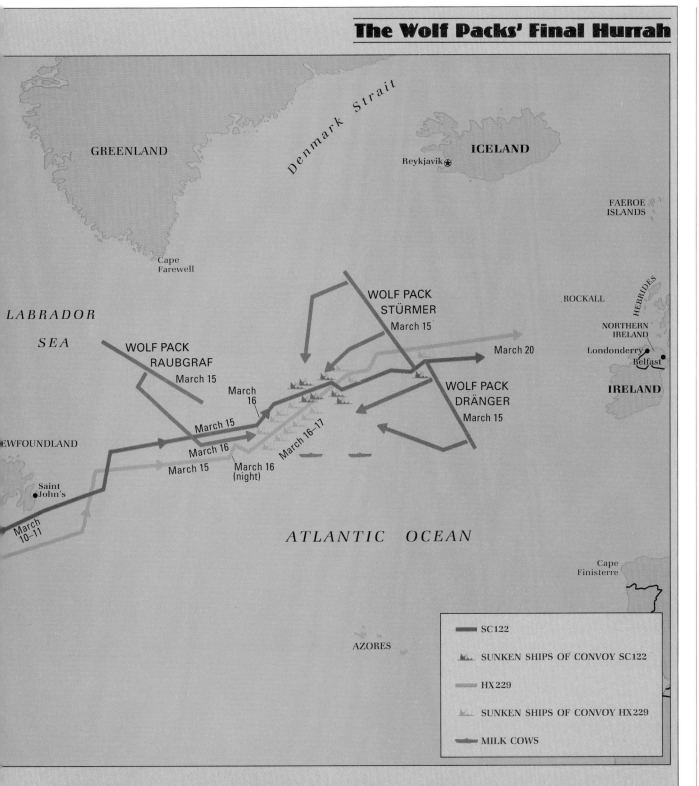

GREENLAND

Denmark Strait

ICELAND

Reykjavík ⊛

FAEROE
ISLANDS

Cape
Farewell

LABRADOR

SEA

ROCKALL

HEBRIDES

WOLF PACK
STÜRMER
March 15

NORTHERN
IRELAND
Londonderry

March 20

Belfast

WOLF PACK
RAUBGRAF
March 15

IRELAND

March
16

WOLF PACK
DRÄNGER
March 15

EWFOUNDLAND

March 15

March 16–17

March 16

Saint
John's

March 15

March 16
(night)

ATLANTIC   OCEAN

March
10–11

Cape
Finisterre

AZORES

▬▬▬ SC 122

🛶 SUNKEN SHIPS OF CONVOY SC 122

▬▬▬ HX 229

🛶 SUNKEN SHIPS OF CONVOY HX 229

🚤 MILK COWS

The map above traces the climax of the U-boat war, a running battle in the Atlantic between three wolf packs and two huge convoys in March of 1943. The westernmost pack deployed by Dönitz—the *Raubgraf*, or Robber Baron, pack—failed to close with the Britain-bound convoys but radioed their position and hurried in pursuit. The *Dränger*, or Harrier, pack, however, lay directly in the path of convoys SC122 and HX229—and safely in the midocean gap, beyond the reach of land-based Allied planes. For three nights, the eleven Dränger U-boats, some refueled and rearmed by supply submarines, torpedoed the convoys while elements of the *Stürmer*, or Daredevil, pack closed in from the north. The swarming U-boats sank one-fourth of the eighty-eight merchant vessels, halting their attacks only after the surviving freighters had reached the protective cover of long-range bombers from Northern Ireland.

ward. The U-603 had claimed its third Norwegian ship of the patrol. When one of the convoy's starboard escorts dropped back to pluck survivors of the *Elin K.* from the sea—only the life of a crewman's pet kitten was lost—the Germans struck again from the same vulnerable side. The U-758, under Lieut. Commander Helmut Manseck, who had been shadowing the convoy for more than twelve hours, scored hits on two merchantmen.

Throughout the night, the U-boats swarmed about their targets. Shortly before dawn, Bernhard Zurmhülen's U-600 fired five torpedoes at three different ships. From the deck of the freighter *Irénée du Pont*, Ensign Frank Pilling, an American, saw, "deep under the surface, two streaks of greasy light, parallel, moving fast, coming in at an angle. There was no time to shout a warning. In one instant, there were the tracks; in another, a great shattering crash." Pilling's ship sank, although he was rescued. Other torpedoes found the refrigerator ship *Nariva,* laden with 5,600 tons of meat, and the tanker *Southern Princess*, which exploded like a Roman candle— and brought the night's score to ten ships sunk or disabled.

About 120 miles to the northeast, other flames seared the sky that night, illuminating the convoy SC122. The havoc here was not the work of a swarming pack, as in the fast convoy, but of one bold assailant. The U-338, like a third of the boats deployed in the current operation, was brand-new. Manfred Kinzel, a former Luftwaffe pilot, had taken command after only nine months of submarine experience. The U-338 could claim only one previous sinking, and it was a dubious one. While the boat was being prepared for launching at Emden, several restraining cables had been cut, and it careened down the slipway and crashed into a small riverboat, which promptly went under. The crew members dubbed their new boat the Wild Donkey and painted an appropriate symbol on the conning tower.

On the night of March 16, 1943, Kinzel and his rookie crew were hurrying south from their position in the group Stürmer to join the attack on HX229 when a more immediate target presented itself. Kinzel looked out from the bridge and saw a veritable armada steaming directly at him. Convoy SC122, forming an imposing front eleven columns wide, contained fifty merchant ships. With an escort of two destroyers, five corvettes, and a frigate, it was better protected than the fast convoy. But by slowing down, Kinzel slipped unobserved between the two lead escorts stationed on the flanks.

At just after 2:00 a.m., the U-338 reached a position a mile in front of the convoy and prepared to fire. Kinzel and his watch officer, Lieutenant Herbert Zeissler, had to improvise because heavy seas had crippled the connection between the sighting glass in the conning tower and the torpedo calculator. "We had to make the attack partly by eye and had to aim

Amid the eerie chaos of a wolf pack's nighttime attack, an Allied freighter is silhouetted against the distant glow of burning ships. The convoy's escorts have fired snowflake flares, hoping to spot submarines on the surface.

the torpedoes by turning the boat onto each target," recalled Zeissler. "We fired the first two at the right-hand ship we could see. We then had to turn to port to aim the second pair at the lead ship of the second column." By that time, the U-338 was so close to another ship—less than 200 yards—that Zeissler could see a man walking along the deck with a flashlight.

Three of Kinzel's torpedoes slammed into their intended targets: two cargo ships at the head of their columns. A fourth missed its mark but struck the ship—an old tramp steamer—behind it. Nearby merchantmen fired snowflake flares to light up the area. In the lingering white glow of the rockets, crews on several ships opened up on the submarine with machine guns. The U-338 turned hard to starboard, fired its stern torpedo, and dived to safety. The torpedo went astray, cut diagonally through at least four columns of the convoy, and, after a journey of some six minutes, smashed into a freighter far to the rear. The Wild Donkey had sunk four ships in less than ten minutes. Unaware of their achievement—they had heard only two explosions—Kinzel's crewmen celebrated with a special breakfast of sausage and strawberries and cream. While they ate, in the cruel manner of war, forty British and Dutch seamen died in the icy sea above them.

Later that morning, SC122 and the six U-boats now shadowing it reached the eastern edge of the air gap. The first four-engine Liberator from Northern Ireland, 900 miles to the east, arrived about 9:00 a.m. and began flying protective cover. But there was a two-hour space between patrols. Once the first Liberator, stretching its fuel capacity to the limit, departed for home shortly after noon, Kinzel saw his opening. He moved the U-338 into position for an underwater attack on the port side of the convoy. He fired three torpedoes in salvo, and one of them hit home. Most of the forty-six-man crew of a Panamanian freighter was sitting down to a lunch of roast chicken when the torpedo exploded, breaking the freighter in two. Two escort vessels—a corvette and a destroyer—raced after the assailant. Kinzel took his boat down to 654 feet, a risky depth, but 100 feet below the maximum setting on conventional depth charges. There his crew celebrated its fifth kill in less than twelve hours, as barrage after barrage of depth charges—twenty-seven in all—exploded harmlessly above them.

That same day, less than 100 miles to the southwest, the fast convoy HX229 also steamed out of the air gap. Before any land-based planes came to its aid, however, the U-384 knocked off two freighters. As the convoys sailed closer to the British Isles, their air cover thickened. Swooping so low that their wings nearly touched the waves, the planes played lethal tag with the U-boats by day, and the surface escorts—strengthened by new arrivals—harassed them by night.

By the morning of March 19, the third day of the battle, the convoys were only 600 miles from friendly bases, and the RAF could provide the services of seven long-range squadrons made up of three types of aircraft—Liberators, Sunderlands, and Flying Fortresses. It was a Fortress that caught the U-384 on the surface, hiding in a squall astern of the slow convoy. Before the U-boat could dive, four depth charges exploded around the boat, and it went down with all forty-seven officers and men aboard.

One easy picking remained for the Germans—the *Matthew Luckenbach*, an American freighter, traveling unescorted in the stretch of sea between the fast and slow convoys. The *Luckenbach* had vacated its place in HX229 the night before, after the captain and his sixty-seven-man crew, apprehensively watching merchantmen go down on either side of their ship, had held a meeting and decided they stood a better chance to survive by steaming ahead at full throttle, or fifteen knots—about six knots faster than the convoy's best speed. The U-527, skippered by Lieut. Commander Herbert Uhlig, was running submerged when the freighter appeared in its periscope. Uhlig miscalculated the range at 1,800 yards, less than half the actual distance of 4,000 yards. But his aim was straight, and two of the three torpedoes he fired caught up with the *Luckenbach*. Responding to the freighter's distress signal, coastguardsmen aboard an American cutter with the slow convoy came back to rescue all hands and presumably lecture the captain on the wisdom of staying with the convoy.

The *Luckenbach* was crippled but afloat, and Uhlig, on his initial patrol, was eager to finish off his first kill. Submerged, he waited until the surface was clear that evening, then moved in. "Only a few moments before my command to fire," Uhlig recalled, "she was hit by the torpedo of another boat and sank rapidly." The *Luckenbach* was the twenty-first and final ship to go down in the epic shootout, which had raged for four days across 600 miles of ocean and cost the Allies a record 141,000 tons of shipping.

At daybreak on March 20, the dozen or so U-boats still in contact with the convoys broke off under orders from Dönitz and headed home. Sailing into the Bay of Biscay, Kinzel's Wild Donkey, victor over five ships and survivor of scores of depth charges, capped its maiden patrol by gunning down a British Halifax bomber. Members of the crew fished the survivor, the flight engineer, out of the water and took him to Saint-Nazaire, a living trophy to go with the triangular white pennants that signaled their triumphs. Dönitz hailed the performance of the Wild Donkey and its companions as the "greatest success ever achieved in a single convoy battle."

For the Allies, the crippling of HX229 and SC122 brought the future of the convoy system into crisis. Ninety-seven ships, a staggering total of 500,000 tons, had been lost during the first three weeks of March—nearly twice the amount that the Allies could build in the same length of time. Worse, two-thirds of the ships were sunk while in convoy. With the linchpin of Allied maritime strategy in jeopardy, the British Admiralty seemed justified in declaring that "the Germans never came so near to disrupting communication between the New World and the Old as in the first twenty days of March 1943." Yet the wolf-pack successes were illusory. According to Dönitz's own yardstick of Allied tonnage sunk per U-boat per day at sea, the results could not compare to those of the Happy Time of 1940. In fact, the March 1943 destruction had been achieved under optimal conditions. Any hope that the U-boats aroused in Berlin was soon to be dashed by the growing superiority of Allied technology and material resources.

Even as his U-boats racked up victories, ominous reports funneled into Dönitz's headquarters. One of the most disturbing described the Allies' newfound ability to locate surfaced U-boats in any weather and at any time of day or night. The Metox radar detectors no longer properly warned of imminent attack, and Dönitz surmised that enemy aircraft and escort ships possessed a new, more powerful radar. To avoid it, he ordered his U-boats leaving and entering the Bay of Biscay to remain submerged even at night.

Dönitz's hunch was correct, although the technical details eluded his experts until late summer. The new radar could clearly register surfaced U-boats at a range of up to twelve miles. And it worked on wavelengths of between 9 and 10 centimeters—not only much shorter than the 1.5-meter wavelength that Metox had been built to detect, but shorter than the German scientists thought possible.

Radar could not explain, however, the Allies' apparent ability to locate the wolf packs at great distances. The repeated rerouting of convoys—move and countermove in what Dönitz called "this game of chess"—indicated special knowledge of German intentions. He knew from reading his cryptographers' intercepts of British radio code that the enemy had accurate information on the whereabouts of his boats. Dönitz suspected treason and had all his staff officers investigated. The probe uncovered several indiscreet French liaisons but no traitors. He still had no idea that one of the culprits was Britain's sophisticated ship- and shore-based high-frequency direction-finding equipment—Huff-Duff—which picked up U-boat radio traffic and allowed the position of a transmission to be fixed by triangulation. In addition, British cryptographers working in the supersecret Ultra program at Bletchley Park, outside London, had cracked the ciphers of the Enigma code machines and, given enough time, could determine where Dönitz was ordering his U-boats.

Although the admiral failed to realize that the British, in effect, were "reading his mail," he was cautious. The German navy employed several ciphers simultaneously. In January 1942, it switched ciphers for U-boats operating in the Atlantic from Hydra to Triton, baffling even the boffins of Bletchley Park. Then, on March 8, 1943, a week before the battle with the two convoys, Dönitz began using Enigma machines that had a fourth coding cylinder, quadrupling the possible rotor sequences. The British code breakers, working with new electronic machines that were forerunners of the digital computer, solved the problem in just ten days, though not in time to prevent the debacles of HX229 and SC122.

Improved Allied weapons technology and the vast American production capacity also confronted every U-boat captain. Convoy escort groups were becoming bigger and better equipped. More of them, for example, were armed with the Hedgehog, a mortarlike weapon that could hurl twenty-four projectiles 250 yards ahead of the ship. In contrast to conventional depth charges, these thirty-two-pound bombs exploded only on contact with a submarine or the sea bottom. This feature eliminated the problem of estimating the target's depth and, since the misses did not churn up the waters nearby, made it possible to immediately regain sonar contact.

The air gap in the mid-Atlantic was shrinking. Liberators fitted with extra fuel tanks could now stay aloft up to sixteen hours, and their numbers were increasing—from twenty planes over the North Atlantic at the end of March to seventy in May. But it was ship-borne aircraft that would squeeze the gap shut. The Allies had begun fitting some merchant ships and tankers with flight decks that could launch and land fighter planes. And in March, the first of the true escort carriers, the USS *Bogue*, a converted merchant-

A U-boat's gun crew, with one man cradling an 88-mm shell, watches a British tanker's final plunge. Torpedoed but refusing to sink, the vessel had to be finished off by the German submarine's powerful deck gun.

man bearing twelve fighters and nine torpedo bombers, made its debut.

Soon aircraft carriers joined destroyers and other antisubmarine vessels in a new kind of flotilla known as a support group. Unlike the escort groups, which sailed with the convoy, the five or six ships in these mobile strike forces could freelance. They would race to the aid of a convoy in trouble, reinforce the escort group, and then break free to chase the attacking U-boats—a capability that earned them the sobriquet "hunter-killers."

As early as April of 1943, the growing Allied capabilities began to pay off. A week-long action against an American convoy bound for the Mediterranean sank only four merchant ships—a fraction of what might have been lost earlier. The Germans' total score for April was respectable—fifty-six ships of 328,000 tons—but only about half of the March toll. The record performance of the U-515, under Lieut. Commander Werner Henke, relieved Dönitz's disappointment somewhat. Operating as a lone wolf off the

One of the first escort carriers, HMS *Battler*, rides at anchor in May 1943. The *Battler* and its sister carriers were makeshift vessels—flight decks bolted onto freighter hulls—that accommodated only a few obsolescent Swordfish torpedo planes (*right*). The carriers proved so effective, however, that twenty-three were built in American yards.

coast of West Africa on the rain-blurred night of April 30, Henke penetrated a fourteen-ship convoy, slipping its heavy escort of three destroyers and five other armed craft. In two attacks over nine hours, Henke and his crew disposed of eight merchantmen totaling 50,000 tons. The wolf packs would require all the cunning and valor of veterans such as Henke, because May brought a fresh crisis in the undecided campaign to dominate the sea.

For Germany, the month began with high hopes of overcoming the strengthened Allied convoys. On May 1, Dönitz had on station in the North Atlantic the most submarines ever—sixty U-boats in four extended patrol lines. Three convoys managed to sail around them. But on the afternoon of May 4, the westward-bound convoy ONS5, in ballast after delivering its

Near the Azores in June 1943, an aerial depth charge hits the U-118. Caught by planes from the carrier USS *Bogue*, the submarine

zigzagged, trying to evade the strafing and bombing that churns the sea around it. The boat sank with forty of its fifty-five men.

cargo to English ports, steamed directly into the middle of a patrol line.

Conditions seemed highly favorable for the Germans. Forty-one U-boats lurked within striking distance, and the merchant ships appeared unusually vulnerable. A gale had scattered the convoy's forty-odd ships, and the ranks of its escorts had been depleted when some of them ran low on fuel and had to head for Newfoundland. Like sharks drawn to blood, the U-boats pounced, sinking five ships that night and four more the next day. The following evening, in a pack now swollen to thirty, they swarmed around the fragmented convoy to deliver what one of the escort captains feared would be "certain annihilation."

Before darkness fell, however, a thick fog set in and the tables turned. The U-boats groped blindly for targets while the escort vessels pinpointed the submarines on their new 10-cm radar screens. The escorts attacked with such fury that four U-boats were lost—two by ramming and two to depth charges—and three more were heavily damaged. The following day, May 6, long-range aircraft and a fresh support group arrived from Newfoundland, and three additional U-boats went to the bottom.

Down seven submarines, Dönitz ordered a new picket line formed south of Greenland to waylay two eastbound convoys. On May 11, his U-boats bagged three stragglers from convoy HX237, and then went after the main body. But HX237 sailed under formidable protection: the usual escorts plus land-based planes and a new support group centered on the British aircraft carrier *Biter*. That day and the next, no U-boat penetrated the protective cordon, and three were destroyed while trying. In each instance, surface ships delivered the knockout blows, but they were alerted by the sentinels overhead—a Sunderland flying boat and the carrier-based Swordfish torpedo bombers—homing in by sight and radar.

The hunter-killer group then sailed westward to assist convoy SC129, which had been under attack for two days. The contest pitted eighteen U-boats, including aces such as Siegfried von Forstner, who as recently as February had scored seven victories in one day, against British Escort Group B2, led by Commander Donald MacIntyre. A skilled submarine-hunter, MacIntyre already numbered Otto Kretschmer's U-99 and Joachim Schepke's U-100 among his victims. No convoy under his protection had ever lost a ship. Forstner ruined that record in an underwater attack before dark on May 11, when he claimed two freighters before depth charges damaged his boat and drove him off.

Later that night, another member of the pack, the U-223, under Lieut. Commander Karl-Jürgen Wächter, engaged MacIntyre in one of the most extraordinary duels of the war. The U-223 was approaching the convoy from astern when MacIntyre's command ship, the destroyer *Hesperus*,

Battered but still afloat, the U-333 returns to its French port after a British frigate depth-charged it and rammed its conning tower. The captain who nursed the boat home called it a "heap of scrap."

located it on radar, then attacked. Wächter dived, but it was too late. MacIntyre, peering through the binoculars he had taken from Kretschmer as a prize of war, spotted the submarine's wake and let loose his depth charges.

The explosives punished the U-223 so severely that it plunged almost out of control. Wächter decided to surface and fight it out. His crew manned the deck guns, but the *Hesperus*, its own guns blazing, closed in and tossed out depth charges with shallow settings. Soon the U-boat wallowed helplessly in the water. Wächter cleared the bridge and began firing torpedoes. But the *Hesperus* was attacking bow on, presenting the smallest-possible target, and the torpedoes flashed harmlessly by. Finally, in desperation, Wächter tried to ram the British destroyer.

MacIntyre also wanted to ram his adversary. But his last experience with that tactic, the successful ramming of a U-boat the previous December, had put the destroyer in drydock for three months of repairs. This time, he elected to try to roll over the submarine by gently nosing up to it and then pushing. The destroyer's bow slid along the hull, tipping the U-boat but not endangering it. Wächter, however, thought his vessel was doomed and ordered all hands on deck. Watching from the *Hesperus*, MacIntyre saw a wounded German sailor fall overboard and a second one jump. He, too, concluded that the U-boat was sinking and returned to the convoy. Both Wächter and MacIntyre were wrong. The crewmen of the U-223 patched their boat and negotiated the twelve-day journey back to Saint-Nazaire.

Despite the U-223's miraculous survival, the arithmetic no longer favored the Atlantic wolf packs. The operation against SC129 cost Dönitz two submarines, one for each Allied ship that went down. A week later, the ratio worsened. In the space of three days, three different convoys sailed through German patrol lines without losing a ship and, in the process, sent five U-boats to the bottom. Listening to the sketchy radio reports in Berlin, Dönitz maintained his dogged determination. He fired off a radio message exhorting his commanders to fulfill their mission: "If there is anyone who thinks that combating convoys is no longer possible, he is a weakling and no true U-boat captain. The Battle of the Atlantic gets harder, but it is the decisive campaign of the war. Be aware of your high responsibility."

A few days later, however, Dönitz counted up the toll and made a painful decision. He knew that at least thirty-one submarines had been lost during the first three weeks of the month. The actual count was thirty-four, and the final toll for all of May, forty-one—nearly three times the loss in any previous month. Among the more than 1,000 casualties were some of the admiral's finest crews and his own son, Peter, who was only twenty-one years old. He had gone down with the U-954 in its maiden action against SC130 on May 19. (Dönitz's older son, Klaus, training to be a navy doctor, was killed a year later, when the mine-laying ship he was on was sunk off the coast of France.) U-boat losses, Dönitz decided, had "reached an intolerable level. Wolf-pack operations against convoys in the North Atlantic were no longer possible."

On May 24—eight weeks and three days after his concerted March offensive had threatened the future of the Allied lifeline—Dönitz pulled the wolf packs out of the North Atlantic. A scattered few German boats would

Blindfolded so they could not observe classified equipment, survivors of a sunken U-boat await transfer from the British destroyer that fished them from the sea. About 7,000 submariners were captured and interned in Britain and North America.

remain in order to give the enemy the impression of a continuing presence, but all the rest were relocated to the area southwest of the Azores.

A week later, Dönitz reported at Hitler's Bavarian retreat, the Berghof. It was a measure of their relationship that the Führer did not reproach him for the U-boat predicament in the North Atlantic. The grand admiral believed the setback to be only temporary and promised to resume the campaign as soon as possible. As a result, Dönitz gained most of what he came for. He won Hitler's support for an increase in production from thirty to forty U-boats a month and for measures intended to counter the Allies' technological edge. The only boost Dönitz did not get was one that Hitler in 1943 could no longer give: planes and pilots for a separate air arm to protect the U-boats and seek out Allied convoys.

By summer, Dönitz was putting his countermeasures into effect. One set of changes improved armaments. To enhance the accuracy of torpedoes, he introduced a new acoustic model known as the T5, or Zaunkönig (literally, wren), which homed in on the noise of a ship's propeller. And to decrease the vulnerability of his boats to air attacks, he added a second gun platform to the deck aft of the conning tower and installed four 20-mm antiaircraft guns there. Some boats received even more guns and were designated "aircraft traps." Their assignment was to patrol transit routes in and out of the Bay of Biscay, deliberately attract enemy aircraft, and shoot it out with them. These specially armed submarines found plenty of Allied planes but downed few of them and suffered heavy casualties. With the North Atlantic bereft of the wolf packs, so many Liberators, Sunderlands, and other planes were free to cover the Bay of Biscay that the U-boat crews dubbed it the *Selbstmordstrecke*, or suicide stretch. "We ran with our decks awash, our bow and stern buoyancy tanks preflooded for instant diving, and our hearts in our mouths," one veteran recalled. "Every hour we spent in our nightmarish passage through these dangerous waters was likely to be our last one." So many U-boats were lost—nearly one a day in late July—that on August 2, Dönitz temporarily halted all sailings in the bay.

The shortcomings of the shootout tactics illustrated the importance of the countermeasure Dönitz sought: a solution to the radar problem. German radar research had suffered enormously from Hitler's 1940 edict banning the development of weapons systems that could not be completed within one year. Refinement of a detector for the British 10-cm radar was further hampered by the refusal of German experts to accept its existence. A captured British pilot reinforced the notion that radar could not operate at such short wavelengths by perpetrating a hoax. There was no new radar, he told his captors; Allied planes and ships were simply homing in on radiation emitted by the Metox detectors on the U-boats. The Metox, in fact, did not give off such emissions, but for a time, many U-boat captains believed the ruse and abandoned use of the detector.

Under Dönitz's prodding, German scientists began to come to grips with the problem of radar and other detection methods during 1943. They developed so-called foxing devices that fooled detectors and led the enemy on wild-goose chases. The Aphrodite, for example, was designed to be deployed from a U-boat and hover just above the water. It consisted of a small balloon affixed to a float. Draped with aluminum foil that stretched out like branches on a tree, the contraption produced echoes resembling those of a U-boat conning tower. Another decoy was a chemical cartridge named Bold (from the word *Kobold*, a deceiving spirit in German folklore). When discharged from a submerged U-boat, it generated so much bubbly hydrogen gas that enemy sonar mistook the pings for a submarine.

The scientists' main accomplishments, however, were devices to detect the Allied 10-cm radar. In August, they reconstructed a radar set taken from a British bomber shot down over Rotterdam six months earlier. Almost immediately, a new detector, built by the Hagenuk company of Kiel, was installed on U-boats as a stopgap. Two months later, the Telefunken company produced a receiver—the Naxos—that could detect both short and long waves up to six miles away and quickly replaced all other receivers.

In September 1943, Dönitz sent his wolf packs back to the North Atlantic armed with new guns, torpedoes, radar detectors, and high expectations. "The Führer is following every phase of your battle," he radioed his commanders. "Attack! Go to it! Sink them!" And indeed, in the first major engagement, a four-day battle with two convoys beginning September 20, a pack of nineteen boats met with great success. They sank ship after ship with their Zaunkönig acoustic torpedoes, reporting afterward a toll of nine merchantmen and twelve escort vessels. News of the destruction of a dozen escort vessels elated Dönitz, because the Zaunkönig had been designed to strip away the convoy's protective cordon. The report also turned out to be erroneous. Only three escorts had actually gone down. The commanders had not meant to inflate their kills; they simply could not remain on the surface to watch the results of their efforts. After firing an acoustic torpedo, standard procedure called for a U-boat to dive to a depth of 200 feet. Hence the skippers were generally too deep to observe the results. Many of the explosions that were mistaken for impact with escort ships were depth charges or torpedoes that had detonated for other reasons.

The battle had demonstrated that the Allies could match any German advance in technology. Allied aircraft, it turned out, now carried their own version of the acoustic torpedo, the Mark-24 mine, known as Fido. Such a

Heinz Rehse, engineering petty officer on the U-511 *(shown above in a prewar photograph)*, brought back this picture album as a memento of his Japanese trip.

Odyssey to the Orient

Hoping to spur Japan's modest undersea fleet to sink more Allied shipping in the Pacific, Hitler gave his Axis ally two of Germany's most advanced submarines. For one of the boats, a Type IXC designated the U-511, the result was a voyage that took the crew halfway around the world to an alien land with no sure way to get home. Their adventure, dubbed Operation Marco Polo, was recorded in a photo album *(above)* that was presented to Heinz Rehse, an engineer on the U-511, by his newfound Japanese friends. Snapshots from the album appear on the following pages.

Leaving Lorient on May 10, 1943, the U-511 spent a month sailing down the west coast of Africa and around the Cape of Good Hope, and another thirty days crossing the Indian Ocean under a blazing sun

that turned the inside of the submarine's steel hull into a steam bath. On July 16, the Germans gratefully nosed the U-511 into the shaded port of Penang, in Japanese-controlled Malaya, where a band serenaded them with an Oriental-flavored treatment of "Deutschland, Deutschland über alles," the German national anthem.

After a brief stop at Singapore, the U-511 crossed the South China Sea and finally reached the Japanese naval base at Kure on August 8, almost three months after leaving France. In the subsequent weeks, the German seamen enjoyed mingling with their Japanese hosts as they struggled to teach a Japanese crew—despite the language barrier—to operate their boat. A banquet celebrated the formal turnover of command. "It feels funny," wrote

Rehse in his diary, "to see the Japanese flag fly on the conning tower instead of the German one."

Now the Germans had to get home. They took over an Italian submarine that had been stranded in Singapore and made it halfway across the Indian Ocean before learning that the tankers that were supposed to refuel them had been sunk. Frustrated, they turned back to exotic Penang. For the rest of the war, they operated the Italian submarine as a cargo vessel, ferrying vital goods to Japan from the edges of its embattled empire.

Two of the Germans died of malaria, but Rehse and most of his mates finally found transport back to their homes and families in 1947, four years after they had set sail on their Oriental odyssey and two years after the war had ended.

A Japanese launch delivers fresh fruit, a rare treat, to the U-511 on its arrival at Penang in July 1943, after two months at sea.

Under the Rising Sun and an incorrectly hung German battle flag, submariners of two nations observe the turning over of the U-511 to Japan at a dinner in the judo training hall on the naval base located outside Kure.

During indoctrination, German and Japanese crews are photographed being ferried to their sub.

Turning the tables at a beach party, a trainee gives Rehse *(right)* **a lesson in Japanese wrestling.**

missile ended the third combat cruise and brief career of Manfred Kinzel and his U-338, the Wild Donkey. The wolf packs continued their campaign against the convoys that autumn, but with even less success. Another German hero, Siegfried von Forstner of the U-402, fell victim to Fido. On October 13, after more than five weeks at sea, he was heading on the surface for a rendezvous with a milk cow to replenish his fuel when planes from an American carrier drove him underwater with depth charges and then delivered the death blow with the air-dropped Fido.

The new German armaments turned out to be mixed blessings. The Zaunkönig torpedoes often proved worthless after the Allies discovered that they operated on a certain sound frequency. If the ship captains slowed down or speeded up their vessels, the torpedoes would swish by harmlessly in search of the special frequency. Later, the Allies found another way to fool the Zaunkönig: a noise-making buoy. When towed by a ship, the device generated more racket than the ship's engines and thus attracted the torpedo. The U-boat's strengthened deck armaments sometimes were a detriment. Even with the extra guns, a submarine was no match for most aircraft. When Dönitz ordered one wolf pack to stay on the surface and fight it out with Allied planes, he lost six boats. Worst of all, his patrol lines were having trouble finding targets; the British had revamped their radio cipher systems the previous June, depriving B-Dienst of information on convoy routings.

Everywhere Dönitz looked during that autumn of 1943, his U-boat war

Its camouflaged snorkel head *(right)* trailing two extended periscopes, a U-boat runs swiftly just below the surface on a shakedown cruise in calm waters. The snorkel's air-intake and exhaust valves allowed a submarine to use its powerful diesel engines while submerged.

was foundering. He dispatched wolf packs to the convoy routes off the coast of South Africa and in the Indian Ocean and, implementing a strategic decision made in 1941, sent a dozen submarines on a mission to Japan to ferry back rubber and other scarce raw materials. But of the thirty-six German U-boats he dispatched to the Far East, only four would return to Germany. The steady destruction of the U-boat tankers, which refueled and replenished the boats at sea, made these distant operations more difficult. Of the fleet of ten type-XIV milk cows, only two survived the year.

By the end of 1943, more U-boats were being lost than Allied ships. Only once more, during the following March, would the boats sink more than 100,000 tons in a month. "An iron year lies behind us," proclaimed Dönitz in his New Year's greeting to the navy. "It has made us Germans hard as no generation before us." But to conserve his shrinking crews and vessels, he had no choice but to abandon the group tactics and deploy his boats singly on lonely, dangerous patrols.

Dönitz recognized that "surface warfare for U-boats had come to an end." What he desperately wanted and was waiting for as 1944 began was a true submarine instead of a mere submersible—a vessel that could travel rapidly underwater, stay there for weeks, and attack while submerged. Such a submarine—a compromise version of the long-proposed Walter boat— had been under development since the previous summer. Dönitz had approved its construction in July, realizing that the Walter boat, with its volatile hydrogen peroxide propulsion system, might take years to perfect.

The electroboat, as it was dubbed, represented a new stage in submarine development. It adopted Helmuth Walter's streamlined double hull but operated on conventional diesel and electric engines. The second hull, which stored fuel in the Walter boat, enabled the electroboat to triple its bank of storage batteries, increasing not only underwater speed but the length of time the vessel could travel submerged.

Another innovative device, called the *Schnorchel*, or snorkel, was a collapsible mast with two tubes that protruded just above the water. The tubes made it possible both to run the diesels to propel the boat and to recharge batteries for the electric engines while submerged at periscope depth. Fresh air to feed the diesels and ventilate the boat came in one tube, and exhaust gases went out the other.

To build the new boat, Albert Speer launched a crash program based on the prefabrication techniques that the Americans had pioneered to build the merchantmen they called Liberty Ships. Each submarine was constructed in eight separate sections, which were manufactured individually at eleven different sites. The sections were then transported to shipyards at Hamburg, Bremen, and Danzig for assembly. Prefabrication cut construction time almost in half. Even so, no electroboat was expected to be ready to go to war for nearly a year.

As a stopgap, Dönitz ordered his technicians to fit out existing U-boats with the snorkel. It was an improvement but not a panacea. Though covered with foam rubber to absorb radar impulses, the protruding head of the snorkel stirred up a trail of foam and exhaust gases that could be spotted in the daytime from the air. And U-boats at periscope depth had to travel slower than six knots to avoid breaking the snorkel off.

During trial runs, a problem cropped up in the float valve in the snorkel's head. This mechanism was designed to keep out water and let in air. But in rough seas, the valve tended to jam closed, cutting off the flow of air. The engines, if not shut down immediately, then sucked the air out of the boat, creating a partial vacuum that left the men gasping for oxygen and sometimes damaged their eardrums when the air pressure finally equalized. If a U-boat developed diesel engine trouble while snorkeling, carbon monoxide fumes could incapacitate, and even kill, the crew members.

The men were willing to trade these problems for a measurable increase in their chances for survival. They could submerge by day, operating electrically on freshly recharged batteries, and then snorkel at night, safely out of reach of the hundreds of Allied planes that now patrolled the Atlantic. If need be, they could stay off the surface for weeks. One boat established a wartime endurance record of sixty-nine days underwater.

Only a portion of the U-boat fleet could be equipped with snorkels before the Allied invasion of western Europe, expected in the spring of 1944. Dönitz prepared to oppose the assault with every means at hand. He ordered the nearly sixty U-boats at bases in Norway and France to stand ready to converge on the invasion armada: "Every vessel taking part in the landing, even if it has but a handful of men or a solitary tank aboard, is a target of the utmost importance that must be attacked regardless of risk."

To many of his commanders, the orders sounded desperate, even suicidal. By some accounts, staff officers who briefed the commanders and crews interpreted the instructions to mean that the U-boats were to ram the enemy ships as a last resort. Harald Busch, a war correspondent assigned to the U-boat branch, later wrote that few men took this interpretation to heart. Busch recalled that the submariners adopted a prudent motto for the invasion: "He who surfaces is sunk!"

The immense fleet of ships and landing craft that shuttled back and forth across the English Channel on D-Day—June 6, 1944—presented the most tempting targets in the history of submarine warfare. Some 4,200 vessels carrying men and supplies plied the narrow waters between England and

A Captain's Death at Sea

The photographs below illustrate the brief lifespan of most German U-boats and their crews. Less than ten months after Lieutenant Hans Steen had taken command of the newly commissioned U-233 in September 1943 *(below, left)*—and before he could record his first kill—an American hunter-killer group caught and depth-charged his boat. Destroyers forced the U-233 to surface, then rammed and shelled it. A direct hit on the conning tower hurled Steen, badly wounded, into the sea. Rescued by the carrier *Card* *(below, right)*, Steen received medical care but died a day later and was buried at sea *(bottom)*.

Skipper Hans Steen stands between two of his crewmen.

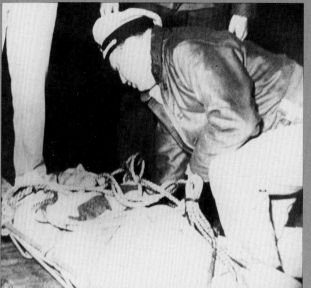

On the USS *Card,* an officer tends the wounded Steen.

In a time-honored ceremony for those who die at sea, Americans commit the German officer to the deep on July 7, 1944.

the Normandy beaches. But hundreds of Allied warships and thousands of planes prevented the U-boats from even getting near them. Day and night, patrols overflew every square mile of the Channel and surrounding waters at least once every thirty minutes.

Only those U-boats with snorkels could remain submerged and survive the first few days of action. The others were sunk, damaged, or forced to turn away. It was June 15 before snorkel-equipped boats scored the first meager successes, sinking two frigates and a landing craft.

Late in August, advancing Allied armies forced the U-boats to evacuate bases on the Bay of Biscay and retreat to Norway. Thanks to the snorkel, all thirty boats ordered there safely made the passage around Ireland and Scotland. But the summer's dispiriting statistics summed up the increasing futility of U-boat warfare. Between D-Day and the end of August, the forces deployed against the Allied armada supplying the Normandy invasion sank five escort vessels, twelve merchantmen, and four landing craft while losing twenty boats of their own.

During the following months, the U-boats fared little better. Relocating to Norway lengthened transit times to and from operations, and traveling underwater shortened a boat's time at sea. The submarines now operated mainly in the coastal waters around the British Isles, where five years earlier they had launched their undersea war. All the U-boats here now carried snorkels, and their losses dwindled. But so did sinkings: In October 1944, submarines sent one ship of 7,000 tons to the deep.

Somehow, Dönitz maintained his outward confidence. "Although he seemed worn and weary," wrote a U-boat commander who saw him early in 1945, "he still transmitted that same spark of enthusiasm that had galvanized us when he spoke in our years of triumph." And he could still turn on the optimism for the Führer, raising hopes for the new one-man and two-man midget submarines now being sent on missions that were scarcely less than suicidal.

Dönitz's hope for a last-minute turn of the tide still rested on the speedy new electroboats. Allied bombing raids and what he described as "teething troubles" during their sea trials had delayed construction. Scores of the boats had been built, but it was February 1945 before the first ones were operational. They sailed at once for British waters, where the U-2336 sank two merchantmen. The wolf pack grew to eight boats that operated without losses. But these first electroboats were the smaller, slower Type XXIIIs. With a crew of thirteen and armed with two torpedoes, they could function successfully only in shallow coastal waters.

The electroboat that Dönitz rightly believed would revolutionize sub-

A lone German officer sits apart in a corner of the conning tower as curious U.S. Navy personnel secure his submarine, the U-805, to a tugboat at the Portsmouth, New Hampshire, naval base in May 1945. The U-805 surrendered to American forces a few days earlier, after Germany had capitulated.

marine warfare was the faster, larger Type XXI, which displaced 1,600 tons and could cruise underwater at speeds up to 17.5 knots, more than twice as fast as conventional submarines. The boat could sail to Cape Horn, at the tip of South America, and back again without surfacing or refueling.

In firepower, too, the Type XXI was ahead of its time. Almost twice the size of other submarines, it packed up to twenty-four torpedoes. Helped by a hydraulic loading mechanism, the crew could reload all six bow tubes in twelve minutes, less time than it normally took to reload one tube, and fire as many as eighteen torpedoes in twenty minutes. Its ultrasensitive hydrophones could pick up a target at a distance of fifty miles. And a new sonar device that detected and calculated the range and speed of the target would enable the boat to sail beneath convoys and launch its torpedoes blind from a depth of 150 feet.

The first type-XXI boat became operational on April 30, 1945, when the U-2511 sailed from Bergen, Norway, on its first war cruise. Its conning tower, which had been painted white to make it more difficult to spot from the air, was emblazoned with a snowman in honor of the boat's veteran captain and Dönitz's former operations officer, Lieut. Commander Adalbert Schnee, whose name means snow in German. That day, Hitler committed suicide in his Berlin bunker after rewarding Dönitz for his unquestioning loyalty by bequeathing him the job of Führer.

It was too late. Four days later, at 3:14 p.m. on May 4, Dönitz, who had already begun negotiations with the western Allies, broadcast an order to cease fire to all U-boat commanders. "You have fought like lions," he told his men in his final message the following day. "Unbeaten and unblemished, you lay down your arms after a heroic battle without equal."

Many captains reacted with the same spirit that had enabled them to endure despite appalling casualty rates. Of 1,155 commissioned U-boats, 725 had been lost during the nearly six years of fighting. Of the 35,000 men who had gone to sea, 28,744 lost their lives—a death rate of 82 percent. Now, rather than surrender their submarines, 2 commanders headed for Argentina, 5 set out for Japan, and 221 scuttled their craft.

Commander Schnee and the crew of the U-2511 wrote perhaps the most fitting postscript. A few hours after receiving the cease-fire order, Schnee, just north of the Faeroe Islands, sighted in his periscope the U-boat's most hated enemy, a hunter-killer group—the British cruiser *Norfolk* and four destroyers. Schnee maneuvered to within 500 yards of the cruiser and lined up in a favorable position to fire his bow torpedoes. He had done this many times, but never with such speed and facility. Then, instead of the order to fire, he uttered an oath. Having delivered its mock attack unnoticed by the enemy, the U-2511 surfaced and cruised back to its base. ✚

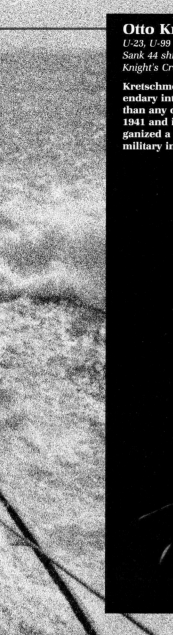

Otto Kretschmer, 1912—
U-23, U-99
Sank 44 ships, 262,203 tons
Knight's Cross, 8/4/40; Oak Leaves, 10/4/40; Swords, 12/26/41

Kretschmer, a professional of legendary intensity, sank more tonnage than any other captain. Captured in 1941 and interned in Canada, he organized a ring of POWs to smuggle military information to Germany.

The U-boat Buccaneers

They were among the most reviled sea captains of all time. The devastation they wrought was fearsome, obliterating 14 million tons of Allied and neutral shipping. One of them, the relentless Otto Kretschmer *(above)*, caused more destruction on the high seas in thirteen months than any commander in history. Even as they gave the world a chilling look at modern warfare—stealthy, technical, and impersonal—the 1,415 men who commanded Germany's U-boats embodied the highest ideals of seafaring warriors. Their seamanship, loyalty to crew and country, and transcendent courage in the face of overwhelming odds won the respect of their bitterest foes. In the end, many of these tough, heroic young men met deaths as harsh as any they had inflicted: 566 boat captains were drowned, asphyxiated, or blown to bits in their grim iron coffins.

Those who eluded death or capture long enough to sink 100,000 tons—and sometimes less, late in the war—earned the Knight's Cross. They owed their success to skill, luck, and the ability to establish bonds with their crews. "We were a band of brothers," said a captain who survived the war. "The success of the commander was not the success of one human being alone, but of all fifty men on board." Sixteen outstanding captains are presented here, with the boats they commanded, ships they sank, and laurels they won.

Johannes Mohr, 1916-1943

U-124
Sank 29 ships, 135,067 tons
Knight's Cross, 3/27/42; Oak Leaves, 1/17/43

Admiral Dönitz called him the "best horse in my stable." Laughing, sunny "Jochen" Mohr was blessed with all the attributes of a perfect U-boat captain: a leadership flair and a zest for combat, tempered by intelligence and an instinctive grasp of U-boat tactics. Mohr also had an irrepressible sense of humor. After torpedoing seven ships during one week in American waters in 1942, he reported to Dönitz in couplets: "The new-moon night is black as ink. / Off Hatteras, the tankers sink / While, sadly, Roosevelt counts the score: / Some 50,000 tons—by Mohr." Mohr's U-124 was itself attacked off Gibraltar on April 3, 1943, and sank with all hands.

Reinhardt Hardegen, 1913—

U-147, U-123
Sank 23 ships, 119,408 tons
Knight's Cross, 1/23/42; Oak Leaves, 4/23/42

The Bremen-born stepson of a renowned World War I submariner, Hardegen channeled an enthusiasm for U-boats into a notable career. On January 12, 1942, he brought the war home to Americans by sinking the steamer *Cyclops* off Cape Cod. Then he scored heavily along the eastern seaboard, destroying seven ships that April. Known as a cold-blooded commander, Hardegen was a jovial music lover. Once the war ended, he declared that "the former enemies are the friends of today" and corresponded with survivors of ships he had sunk.

Heinrich Lehmann-Willenbrock, 1911-1986

U-5, U-96
Sank 25 ships, 183,223 tons
Knight's Cross, 2/26/41; Oak Leaves, 12/31/41

Descended from a family of land-locked farmers, red-haired, young Heinrich Lehmann-Willenbrock gained his first taste of military training in an orphanage outside Berlin. Nicknamed *Recke*, a word meaning valiant warrior in German, he became a consummate seaman and a trusted, unflappable commander. After the war, his exploits were fictionalized in *Das Boot*, a popular novel that was made into an acclaimed motion picture.

Günther Prien, 1908-1941

U-47
Sank 33 ships, 197,218 tons
Knight's Cross, 10/18/39

"I get more fun out of a good convoy exercise than out of any shore leave," remarked Prien. The "Bull of Scapa Flow" became Germany's most idolized naval hero after sinking the battleship *Royal Oak*. Quick-tempered and nonintrospective, he nevertheless wore his wife's scarf into battle and saved fan letters from schoolchildren. His loss in 1941 caused the nation to mourn.

Günther Hessler, 1909-1986

U-107
Sank 20 ships; 113,462 tons
Knight's Cross, 6/24/41; German Cross in Gold, 11/17/44

Hessler had already served fourteen years in the navy when he joined the U-boat arm in 1940, at the age of thirty. He became a deadly marksman, capable of sinking an enemy ship with a single torpedo. He once cruised 22,000 miles in 135 days, sinking fourteen ships—the most successful mission of the war. Married to Dönitz's daughter, Ursula, he joined his father-in-law's staff in 1941 as chief of operations. After the war, he wrote an official history of the U-boat campaign.

Klaus Scholtz, 1909-1987

U-108
Sank 24 ships, 111,546 tons
Knight's Cross, 12/26/41; Oak Leaves, 9/10/42

Growing up in the Baltic port of Danzig, where his father was the lord mayor, imbued Scholtz with an abiding love for the sea. As commander of the U-108 from September 1940 to September 1942, he stalked Allied shipping lanes from Gibraltar to the Caribbean and beyond. Modest and unassuming, he engendered a relaxed atmosphere on his boat and refused to prove his valor by grandstanding. "He never succumbed, as many other captains did, to a fear of his own cowardice," said the U-108's engineering officer. "He could attack successfully, but he could also retreat successfully." Scholtz was commanding officer of the German U-boat flotilla in Bordeaux when the war ended.

Fritz-Julius Lemp, 1913-1941
U-30, U-110
Sank 20 ships, 95,507 tons
Knight's Cross, 8/14/40

Lemp sank the liner *Athenia* as the war began and lost the Enigma machine twenty-one months later. A genial commander, he was highly regarded for tenacity in combat and empathy for his men. Preoccupation with his crew's safety may have doomed his attempt in 1941 to scuttle the U-110 before the British boarded the boat and shot him.

Erich Topp, 1914—
U-57, U-552, U-2513
Sank 35 ships, 192,601 tons
Knight's Cross, 6/20/41; Oak Leaves, 4/11/42; Swords, 8/17/42

His boat was emblazoned with a red devil, and in ten sorties in the North Atlantic and along the coast of the United States, Topp sank more tonnage than all but two of the Reich's captains. Assigned to the tactical training school in Goten-hafen in 1942, he returned three years later as skipper of a new long-range type-XXI boat and was captured by the British at war's end.

Herbert Schultze, 1909-1987

U-48
Sank 27 ships, 174,475 tons
Knight's Cross, 1/3/40; Oak Leaves, 6/12/41

One of the commanders who domi-
nated the Atlantic Ocean in the
war's early months, Schultze was
the first to sink 100,000 tons and the
second—after Prien—to earn the
Knight's Cross. Younger officers
referred to him as *Vaddi*, or Pop, for
his generous, paternal attitude.
Schultze was similarly solicitous
toward the enemy: After sinking the
freighter *Firby* in 1939, he radioed
London to request that the British
send a ship to pick up the survivors.

Hans-Diedrich Freiherr von Tiesenhausen, 1913—

U-331
Sank 2 ships, 40,235 tons
Knight's Cross, 1/27/42

Baron Tiesenhausen, a son of Baltic
German nobility, patrolled the
Mediterranean on eight of his nine
missions. There, in November 1941,
he torpedoed the *Barham*, the only
British battleship to be sunk in
open waters by a U-boat. Twelve
months later, the U-331 itself was
destroyed, leaving fifteen survivors,
including Tiesenhausen, who was
wounded. He was interned for the
rest of the war in Canada. In 1951,
he returned there as an immigrant.

Carl Emmermann, 1918—

U-172
Sank 27 ships, 152,904 tons
Knight's Cross, 11/27/42; Oak Leaves, 7/4/43

A native of Hamburg who joined the navy as a teenager, Emmermann operated as far from home as the Indian Ocean, Cape Town, and the coast of Brazil. In August of 1943, he risked his submarine in order to help rescue the crew of the U-604 after it had been damaged by American aircraft. Surviving the war, he returned to his hometown, studied engineering, and prospered in business.

Wolfgang Lüth, 1913-1945

U-9, U-138, U-43, U-181
Sank 47 ships, 226,671 tons
Knight's Cross, 10/24/40; Oak Leaves, 11/13/42; Swords, 4/15/43;
Diamonds, 8/9/43

Second only to Kretschmer in tonnage sunk, Lüth was one of two submariners to win the Knight's Cross with Oak Leaves, Swords, and Diamonds. Lüth inspired his men with meticulous attention to their comfort, lectures on the Reich's goals, and shipboard contests—but noted that success in combat was the only reliable spirit-lifter: "Crews will always prefer the successful commander, even though he may be a fathead, to the one who is consideration itself but sinks no ships." After fifteen missions, Lüth died in 1945 as commandant of the Naval Academy at Dortmund—shot when he failed to give the password to a sentry at the academy gates.

Joachim Schepke, 1912-1941

U-100
Sank 37 ships, 155,882 tons
Knight's Cross, 9/24/40; Oak Leaves, 12/1/40

Comrades tweakingly dubbed Joachim Schepke, the fair-haired son of a naval officer, "His Majesty's best-looking officer." Unlike the more aloof Kretschmer and Prien, Schepke reveled in the attention he attracted in the heady early days as one of Germany's three most celebrated aces. He accentuated his matinée-idol looks by wearing his cap at a rakish tilt, and he adopted a breezy manner toward superiors— affectations encouraged by Dönitz, who recognized that Schepke's debonair style boosted morale in the U-boat arm. Schepke maintained his élan until the instant of his death in 1941; his last words, shouted before the destroyer *Vanoc* crushed him and the U-100, were reassurances to his crew.

Peter Erich Cremer, 1911—

U-152, U-333, U-2519
Sank 7 ships, 32,724 tons
Knight's Cross, 6/5/42

Initially rejected by the navy be- cause his mother was French and his paternal grandmother British, "Ali" Cremer threw himself into combat despite an inner dismay. "Unlike many young officers, who saw fame and promotion in a trial of arms, the prospect of war did not elate or excite me," he wrote. In 1942, the U-333 was rammed in the Bay of Biscay, and seven men were lost. But Cremer brought the boat to port—giving rise to a slogan his crews recited from then on: "Ali's better than life insurance."

Albrecht Brandi, 1914-1966

U-617, U-380, U-967
Sank 12 ships, 31,689 tons
Knight's Cross, 1/21/42; Oak Leaves, 4/11/43; Swords, 5/9/43; Diamonds, 11/24/44

Persuaded to join the prewar navy by his father, who frowned on his son's ambitions as an architect, Brandi *(surrounded by his crew, below)* became one of the U-boat command's most highly decorated officers—only he and Wolfgang Lüth received the Knight's Cross with Oak Leaves, Swords, and Diamonds. Cheerful and optimistic by nature, Brandi credited his men for his honors. "The commander wears his medals for the crew," he said. In the years after the war, he built a successful career, as an architect.

Acknowledgments and Picture Credits

The editors thank the following individuals and institutions for their help in the preparation of this book: Canada: White Rock—Hans-Diedrich Freiherr von Tiesenhausen. England: London—Karl Wahnig; Alan Williams, Imperial War Museum. Shrewsbury—G. Archer Parfitt, Shropshire Regimental Museum. South Croydon—Brian Leigh Davis. Federal Republic of Germany: Bochum—Ursula Hessler. Bornheim—Friedrich Grade. Bremen—Reinhardt Hardegen. Celle—Carl Emmermann. Cuxhaven—Horst Bredow, U-Boot-Archiv. Dortmund—Franz Kurowski. Eckernförde—Ralf Stender, Marinewaffenschule. Feucht—Helmut Martin. Hinte—Otto Kretschmer. Kiel—Klaus Schaele. Koblenz —Meinrad Nilges, Bundesarchiv. Munich —Elisabeth Heidt, Süddeutscher Verlag Bilderdienst. Remagen—Erich Topp. Stuttgart—Prof. Dr. Jürgen Rohwer, Bibliothek für Zeitgeschichte. Troisdorf—Helmut Haake. Berlin—Heidi Klein, Bildarchiv Preussischer Kulturbesitz; Gabrielle Kohler, Archiv für Kunst und Geschichte; Wolfgang Streubel, Ullstein Bilderdienst. France: Maisons-Alfort—Serge-Antoine Legrand. German Democratic Republic: Berlin—Hannes Quaschinsky, ADN-Zentralbild. Italy: Milan—Erminio Bagnasco, Giancarlo Costa. Rome—Aldo Fuga Casanova S.T.V., Ufficio Storico della Marina Militare. United States of America: Catskill—Heinz Rehse. Chicago—Keith Gill, Terri Sinnott, Museum of Science and Industry. District of Columbia—Elizabeth Hill, National Archives; Eveline Nave, Library of Congress; John C. Riley, Naval Historical Center. Dover—Don Mindemann. Elkhart—Hans Goebeler.

Credits for illustrations from left to right are separated by semicolons, from top to bottom by dashes.
Cover: Ullstein Bilderdienst, West Berlin. 4, 5: ADN-Zentralbild, Berlin, GDR. 6, 7: Ullstein Bilderdienst, West Berlin. 8, 9: Süddeutscher Verlag Bilderdienst, Munich. 10, 11: Ullstein Bilderdienst, West Berlin. 12: UPI/Bettmann Newsphotos. 14: Ullstein Bilderdienst, West Berlin. 17: FPG, Intl., New York. 20: AP/Wide World Photos. 23: From *Die Geschichte des Deutschen Ubootbaus* by Eberhard Rössler, Bernard und Graefe Verlag, Koblenz, 1975. 24: FPG, Intl., New York. 25: Horst Bredow, U-Boot-Archiv, Cuxhaven. 26, 27: Black Star, New York. 28: AP/Wide World Photos. 30: Larry Sherer, courtesy Don Mindemann. 31: AP/Wide World Photos. 33: Maps by R. R. Donnelley and Sons Company, Cartographic Services. 34, 35: Horst Bredow, U-Boot-Archiv, Cuxhaven; UPI/Bettmann Newsphotos—Ullstein Bilderdienst, West Berlin. 36, 37: Art by William J. Hennessy, Jr. 38:

Larry Sherer, courtesy Don Mindemann— art by William J. Hennessy, Jr. 41: Ullstein Bilderdienst, West Berlin. 42, 43: Art by John Batchelor; UPI/Bettmann Newsphotos. 44-57: Art by John Batchelor, photos by Brian Seed, hand-tinted by Tom Kochel, courtesy the Museum of Science and Industry, Chicago. 58: Michael Latil, from *So War der U-Boot-Krieg* by Harald Busch, Verlag K. W. Schütz, Preussisch Oldenburg, 1983. 60, 61: Map by R. R. Donnelley and Sons Company, Cartographic Services. 63-67: Ullstein Bilderdienst, West Berlin. 68, 69: Bundesarchiv, Koblenz. 71: Bundesarchiv, Koblenz —© Fred Dott, Hamburg, courtesy Otto Kretschmer, Hinte. 72, 73: Horst Bredow, U-Boot-Archiv, Cuxhaven—courtesy Don Mindemann. 74: Roger-Viollet, Paris. 75: Ullstein Bilderdienst, West Berlin. 76: ADN-Zentralbild, Berlin, GDR. 77: Ullstein Bilderdienst, West Berlin. 79: Bundesarchiv, Koblenz. 80, 81: UPI/Bettmann Newsphotos; Popperfoto, London—Crown copyright, courtesy the Trustees of the Imperial War Museum, London. 83: Horst Bredow, U-Boot-Archiv, Cuxhaven. 86, 87: Bundesarchiv, Koblenz (3). 88: Giancarlo Costa, Milan. 89: Fred Dott, Hamburg, courtesy U-Boot-Archiv, Cuxhaven. 90, 91: S.I.R.P.A./ E.C.P. Armées, Paris, except bottom left, Ullstein Bilderdienst, West Berlin. 92: Süddeutscher Verlag Bilderdienst, Munich. 93: Horst Bredow, U-Boot-Archiv, Cuxhaven —Ullstein Bilderdienst, West Berlin— Bundesarchiv, Koblenz. 94, 95: Ullstein Bilderdienst, West Berlin; Bundesarchiv, Koblenz (2). 96, 97: Bundesarchiv, Koblenz —ADN-Zentralbild, Berlin, GDR—Bundesarchiv, Koblenz; Ullstein Bilderdienst, West Berlin (2). 98: Bundesarchiv, Koblenz. 99: Michael Latil, from *So War der U-Boot-Krieg* by Harald Busch, Verlag K. W. Schütz, Preussisch Oldenburg, 1983—Ullstein Bilderdienst, West Berlin (2). 100, 101: Fox Movietone News, Inc.; Ullstein Bilderdienst, West Berlin—Bildarchiv Preussischer Kulturbesitz, West Berlin. 102: Michael Latil, from *So War der U-Boot-Krieg* by Harald Busch, Verlag K. W. Schütz, Preussisch Oldenburg, 1983—Bundesarchiv, Koblenz. 103: U-Boot-Archiv, Cuxhaven. 104: Horst Bredow, U-Boot-Archiv, Cuxhaven. 105: Bundesarchiv, Koblenz. 106: National Archives, no. 80-G-63472. 109: Map by R. R. Donnelley and Sons Company, Cartographic Services. 110, 111: Crown copyright, courtesy the Trustees of the Imperial War Museum, London—Ufficio Storico della Marina Militare, Rome. 112, 113: Michael Latil, from *U-Boat Aces and Their Fates* by Geoffrey P. Jones, William Kimber, London, 1988 (4); Ufficio Storico della Marina Militare, Rome, courtesy the Imperial War Museum,

London. 114, 115: Larry Sherer, courtesy Don Mindemann. 116, 117: National Archives, no. 80-G-2183. 118: Horst Bredow, U-Boot-Archiv, Cuxhaven. 120: National Archives, no. 80-G-40330. 121: National Archives, no. 26-G-1583. 123-125: Crown copyright, courtesy the Trustees of the Imperial War Museum, London. 126, 127: AP/Wide World Photos; art by William J. Hennessy, Jr. 129: Bundesarchiv, Koblenz. 130: U-Boot-Archiv, Cuxhaven (2). 134, 135: National Archives. 136, 137: National Archives, no. 80-G-411959—National Archives, no. 80-G-358477. 138, 139: Horst Bredow, U-Boot-Archiv, Cuxhaven (3). 140, 141: Crown copyright, courtesy the Trustees of the Imperial War Museum, London. 142: UPI/Bettmann Newsphotos. 144: Süddeutscher Verlag Bilderdienst, Munich; Derek Bayes, London, courtesy of the K.S.L.I. Museum, Shrewsbury. 146, 147: Horst Bredow, U-Boot-Archiv, Cuxhaven, except top left, Larry Sherer, courtesy Don Mindemann. 149: Bundesarchiv, Koblenz. 150, 151: Map by R. R. Donnelley and Sons Company, Cartographic Services. 153: Crown copyright, courtesy the Trustees of the Imperial War Museum, London. 156: Bildarchiv Preussischer Kulturbesitz, West Berlin. 158, 159: Popperfoto, London (2). 160, 161: National Archives. 163: Bundesarchiv, Koblenz. 164: UPI/Bettmann Newsphotos. 167: Michael Latil, courtesy Heinz Rehse, Catskill, New York; courtesy Heinz Rehse. 168, 169: Michael Latil, courtesy Heinz Rehse, Catskill, New York (4). 170: Süddeutscher Verlag Bilderdienst, Munich. 173: Horst Bredow, U-Boot-Archiv, Cuxhaven (3). 175: UPI/Bettmann Newsphotos. 177: Bundesarchiv, Koblenz, background photo, Ullstein Bilderdienst, West Berlin. 178, 179: Michael Latil, from *So War der U-Boot-Krieg* by Harald Busch, Verlag K. W. Schütz, Preussisch Oldenburg, 1983; National Archives, no. 242-HB-51609; Süddeutscher Verlag Bilderdienst, Munich; UPI/Bettmann Newsphotos, background photo, Ullstein Bilderdienst, West Berlin. 180, 181: Bundesarchiv, Koblenz; Horst Bredow, U-Boot-Archiv, Cuxhaven; Erich Topp, Remagen; Bundesarchiv, Koblenz, background photo, Ullstein Bilderdienst, West Berlin. 182, 183: S.I.R.P.A./E.C.P. Armées, Paris; Michael Latil, from *Ritter der Sieben Meere* by Franz Kurowski, Erich Pabel Verlag, Rastatt, 1963; Horst Bredow, U-Boot-Archiv, Cuxhaven (2), background photo, Ullstein Bilderdienst, West Berlin. 184, 185: Bundesarchiv, Koblenz; UPI/ Bettmann Newsphotos; Michael Latil, from *Ritter der Sieben Meere* by Franz Kurowski, Erich Pabel Verlag, Rastatt, 1963, background photo, Ullstein Bilderdienst, West Berlin.

Bibliography

Books

Angelucci, Enzo, *The Rand McNally Encyclopedia of Military Aircraft, 1914-1980*. New York: Military Press, 1983.

Angolia, John R., *For Führer and Fatherland*. San Jose, Calif.: R. James Bender, 1976.

Bagnasco, Erminio, *Submarines of World War Two*. Annapolis, Md.: Naval Institute Press, 1977.

Beesly, Patrick, "Special Intelligence and the Battle of the Atlantic: The British View." In *Changing Interpretations and New Sources in Naval History*. Ed. by Robert William Love, Jr. New York: Garland, 1980.

Bird, Keith W., *Weimar, the German Naval Officer Corps and the Rise of National Socialism*. Amsterdam: B. R. Grüner, 1977.

Brennecke, Jochen, *The Hunters and the Hunted*. Transl. by R. H. Stevens. New York: W. W. Norton, 1958.

Buchheim, Lothar-Günther, *U-boat War*. Transl. by Gudie Lawaetz. New York: Alfred A. Knopf, 1978.

Busch, Harald, *U-boats at War*. Transl. by L. P. R. Wilson. New York: Ballantine Books, 1955.

Cremer, Peter, *U-boat Commander*. Transl. by Lawrence Wilson. Annapolis, Md.: Naval Institute Press, 1984.

Dönitz, Karl:
The Conduct of the War at Sea. Washington, D.C.: Division of Naval Intelligence, January 15, 1946.
Deutsche Strategie zur See im Zweiten Weltkrieg. Frankfurt: Bernard & Graefe, 1970.
Memoirs. Transl. by R. H. Stevens. Cleveland: World, 1959.

Dörr, Manfred, *Die Ritterkreuzträger der U-Boot-Waffe*. Osnabrück: Biblio, 1988.

Frank, Wolfgang, *The Sea Wolves*. Transl. by R. O. B. Long. New York: Rinehart, 1955.

Gasaway, E. B., *Grey Wolf, Grey Sea*. New York: Ballantine Books, 1970.

Gatzke, Hans W., ed., *European Diplomacy between Two Wars, 1919-1939*. Chicago: Quadrangle Books, 1972.

Haraszti, Éva H., *Treaty-Breakers or "Realpolitiker"?* Boppard, W.Ger.: Harald Boldt, 1974.

Herzog, Bodo, *U-Boote im Einsatz, 1939-1945*. Dorheim, W.Ger.: Podzun, 1970.

Hoyt, Edwin P., *U-boats Offshore*. New York: Stein and Day, 1978.

Hughes, Terry, and John Costello, *The Battle of the Atlantic*. New York: Dial Press/James Wade, 1977.

Jones, Geoffrey P.:
The Month of the Lost U-boats. London: William Kimber, 1977.
U-boat Aces and Their Fates. London: William Kimber, 1988.

Kurowski, Franz:
An Alle Wölfe: Angriff! Friedberg, W.Ger.: Podzun-Pallas, 1986.
Ritter der Sieben Meere. Rastatt, W.Ger: Erich Pabel, 1963.

McMurtrie, Francis E., ed., *Jane's Fighting Ships, 1943-4*. London: Sampson, Low, Marston, 1944.

Mason, David, *U-boat*. New York: Ballantine Books, 1968.

Middlebrook, Martin, *Convoy*. New York: William Morrow, 1977.

Peillard, Léonce, *The Laconia Affair*. Transl. by Oliver Coburn. New York: G. P. Putnam's Sons, 1963.

Price, Alfred, *Aircraft versus Submarine*. London: Jane's, 1980.

Raeder, Erich, *My Life*. Transl. by Henry W. Drexel. Annapolis, Md.: United States Naval Institute, 1960.

Rohwer, Jürgen:
Axis Submarine Successes, 1939-1945. Annapolis, Md.: Naval Institute Press, 1983.
The Critical Convoy Battles of March 1943. Annapolis, Md.: Naval Institute Press, 1977.
"The U-boat War against the Allied Supply Lines," in *Decisive Battles of World War II*. Ed. by H. A. Jacobsen and J. Rohwer, transl. by Edward Fitzgerald. New York: G. P. Putnam's Sons, 1965.
"Ultra and the Battle of the Atlantic: The German View." In *Changing Interpretations and New Sources in Naval History*. Ed. by Robert William Love, Jr. New York: Garland, 1980.

Roskill, S. W.:
The Defensive. Vol. 1 of *The War at Sea, 1939-1945*. London: Her Majesty's Stationery Office, 1954.
The Period of Reluctant Rearmament, 1930-1939. Vol. 2 of *Naval Policy between the Wars*. Annapolis, Md.: Naval Institute Press, 1976.
The Secret Capture. London: Collins, 1959.

Rössler, Eberhard:
Die Torpedos der Deutschen U-Boote. Herford, W.Ger.: Koehlers Verlagsgesellschaft, 1984.
U-boat: The Evolution and Technical History of German Submarines. Transl. by Harold Erenberg. London: Arms and Armour Press, 1981.

Ruge, Friedrich, *Der Seekrieg*. Transl. by M. G. Saunders. Annapolis, Md.: United States Naval Institute, 1957.

Seth, Ronald, *The Fiercest Battle*. London: Hutchinson, 1961.

Showell, Jak P. Mallmann:
The German Navy in World War Two. Annapolis, Md.: Naval Institute Press, 1979.
U-boat Command and the Battle of the Atlantic. London: Conway Maritime Press, 1989.
U-boats under the Swastika. New York: Arco, 1977.

Stern, Robert C., *U-boats in Action*. Carrollton, Tex.: Squadron/Signal, 1977.

Von der Porten, Edward P., *The German Navy in World War II*. New York: Thomas Y. Crowell, 1972.

Waters, John M., Jr., *Bloody Winter*. Annapolis, Md.: Naval Institute Press, 1984.

Werner, Herbert A., *Iron Coffins*. New York: Holt, Rinehart and Winston, 1969.

Westwood, David, *The Type VII U-boat*. Annapolis, Md.: Naval Institute Press, 1984.

Williamson, Gordon, *The Iron Cross*. Poole, England: Blandford Press, 1984.

Wilmot, Chester, *The Struggle for Europe*. New York: Harper & Brothers, 1952.

Periodicals

"Air Raids and Sea Threats Continue to Harass Britain." *Newsweek*, October 30, 1939.

Davis, Brian Leigh, "U-boat Uniforms, 1939-45." 3 parts. *Military Illustrated*, December 1986/January 1987, February/March 1987, June/July 1987.

Decker, Hans Joachim, "404 Days! The War Patrol Life of the German U-505." *United States Naval Institute Proceedings*, March 1960.

Russell, Allard G., and Karl F. W. Gartner, "U-boat Stopped in Atlantic Mining." *All Hands*, February 1985.

"10,000 Tonnen am Horizont." *Signal*, November 1, 1941.

Waters, John M., Jr., "Stay Tough." *United States Naval Institute Proceedings*, December 1966.

Other Publications

National Archives. Files of the Office of the Chief of Naval Operations. Record Group 38. "Report on the Interrogation of Survivors from U-604 and U-185 Sunk 11 August 1943 and 24 August 1943." November 4, 1943.

National Archives. Files of the Office of Naval Intelligence. Record Group 38. Special Activities OP/16-Z. Box 21, 22.

National Archives. Kriegstagebuch des Befehlshabers der Unterseeboote (BdU KTB). October 31, 1939; May 15, 1940.

National Archives. Kriegstagebuch des Führers der Unterseeboote (FdU KTB). August 31, 1939; September 24, 1939; September 28, 1939.

National Archives. Personal Akte Beurteilung. November 1, 1923; November 1, 1925; November 1, 1931; November 1, 1932.

Index

Time-Life Books Inc. offers a wide range of fine recordings, including a *Rock 'n' Roll Era* series. For subscription information, call 1-800-621-7026 or write Time-Life Music, P.O. Box C-32068, Richmond, Virginia 23261-2068.